IN SEARCH OF THE FIGHTER PILOT'S WIFE

BERNIE TERRIFIC

 iUniverse®

IN SEARCH OF THE FIGHTER PILOT'S WIFE

iUniverse books may be ordered through booksellers or by contacting:

iUniverse
1663 Liberty Drive
Bloomington, IN 47403
www.iuniverse.com
1-800-Authors (1-800-288-4677)

ISBN: 978-1-5320-8604-5 (sc)
ISBN: 978-1-5320-8605-2 (e)

Print information available on the last page.

iUniverse rev. date: 10/24/2019

"Straight from a tormented mind- set, a compelling yet brutally honest and disturbingly detailed autobiography of an abused child, written by an abused child… If you or someone that you know was tortured as a child, it would behoove you to take in this relatively short read"…

DEDICATION

On January 24, 2019, 10 year old Mia Kurihara was murdered by her father after revealing in a "child bullying" school survey that she was being beaten daily by her parents. The school administrators had insured the strictest confidence on this matter.

The school betrayed Mia… Instead of notifying CPS, she was turned over to her tormentors. Within 24 hours, she was tortured to death by the very people that had brought her into this world. They each received 25 years.

Of the 1400-2,550 children, annually murdered by their parents, USA stats, one has to wonder how tormented those final little thoughts must have been…

This narrative is dedicated to Mia and to all abused children from all time and continuum...

PREFACE TO
"IN SEARCH OF THE FIGHTER PILOT'S WIFE"

Throughout the annals of time, intelligent design has had His hand in producing millions upon billions of souls. For the sake of propagating our species we have been designed in His image. Our divine Maker in all of His glory intended on giving us a fighting chance of survival. The right to exist. In this enterprise we call life, there are absolutely zero guarantees.

Every now and again, He would produce a Mary Magdalene, a Joan of Arc, a mother Teresa, or Golda Meir. Aside from giving us His very own Son, every once in several millennium he would create a soul, nearly as perfect as his own. Such a soul is a reflection of His perfect love. A love with an incarnate heart which is as unconditional, undying and as selfless as our divine Maker's.

At this moment, a choir of Archangels would sing out in a glorious celestial chorus. On these rare occasions, He would have smiled with a twinkle in His eye. The creation of yet another miraculous masterpiece.

In reality, every life is miraculous. Most of us unceremoniously kerplop into this human enterprise we call life. We fumble our way through our lives with the cards we are dealt. In many cases merely struggling to exist. We are all given the same miraculous bodies. We are given the same miraculous central processing unit, our brain. All for the chance of starting life on an even keel. *The human mind* is as resilient as our flesh and bones. Our Lord, truly is a Master architect and programmer.

As the fighter pilots first born son, I am afforded the opportunity to share from a very personal and early perspective. I was blessed with a rather innate memory. Please allow me to open a window into my heart, baring my soul on matters of my most appalling secrets. I would like to invite you in for a ride, a ride with the fighter pilot's wife at the helm.

In my lifetime I have loved and lost two women to cancer. My wife of nine years, twenty six years ago and now my mother have left an abysmal chasm in my heart. The loss of my wife left me literally breathless. There were times I would sit in solitude with a thousand yard stare. After a while I would start to feel faint as my head would begin to swirl. It was then that I realized I had simply forgotten to breathe.

My new reality was one where my world would be much altered. It has now been nearly four years our since my mother has left us.

The French have a word they use to acknowledge their departed,... "homage". It is my intent to achieve this end. Like a majestic lioness, my mother was one of life's quintessential alpha females with a pronounced contradiction in her character... In many ways, she was larger than life. Inasmuch as our Maker has created only one perfect soul, my mother had a darkside.

Begging your indulgence, as on a roller coaster ride, my journey starts off as in "the calm before the storm". It would eventually build up to a crescendo of sorts. Please allow me to set the stage, from the first person singular. Make certain that all your seat trays are up and your belts are tightly fastened. Please accept this invitation to a front row seat on the ride of my life.

Incidentally, I feel obligated to forewarn you. You *WILL* be exposed to raw, psychological nudity. My life's depictions are disturbingly detailed and brutally honest. It is my intent to paint, in stark reality and with riveting candor, an accurate portrayal. This, a summation of my life's narrative.

By sharing with you vignettes from our lives together, I hope to create a more holistic picture of who "the fighter pilot's wife "was. How we all got to where we are. How it may apply to and benefit you. If in some small way, this adds clarity to your life, then I have succeeded in my wildest dreams.

It is my sincerest desire that you or someone you know and love, may be enlightened. It is with a heavy heart and utmost sincerity that I illustrate how the fighter pilot's wife had influenced her children. While mere words may fall short, it is my intention to convey a series of crystal clear microcosms. Painting an unvarnished portrayal of my life with "the fighter pilot's wife", ... hear her roar!

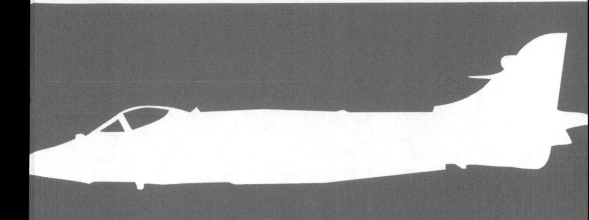

BON VOYAGE

My absolute earliest memory, I was not quite 2 years of age. The year of our Lord, 1956. The setting was the Big Apple. Lt. Fighter pilot, his young wife and three children were boarding an Air France DC 10.

It was a damp, windy night. The icy rain was stinging our faces as we walked and waddled up the ramped stairway to the DC 10's fuselage. I remember the tremendous roaring of the eight DC 10 propelled engines. Their harmonic vibrations made everything vibrate intensely. The lights from the New York skyline stood sole witness to our departure.

My mother was carrying my baby brother, Felix. He was nothing more than a mere tadpole in a baby blanket. My sister Betty, 11 months my senior was present and accounted for.

I remember how narrow the cabin was, maybe four seats across with a narrow aisle down the middle. It was very dimly lit and I could see smoky vapor with every breath I took. "How odd is this?" I thought. Everything I touched buzzed with intensity. I could feel the vibrations in my little chest. A very pleasant woman gave me a balloon penguin to amuse myself.

Then there was this obnoxious businessman, donning a suit and tie, sitting across the aisle from me. He was smiling a lot, drinking penguin scotch and making strange noises at me. Sounded like goo-goo and gaga. I sat there, wide eyed in wonderment. I must have sensed that we were about to embark on something larger than the sum total of ourselves. Next thing I recall, we were in France. The birthplace of our liberty. Thank God for the French!

Having settled into temporary base housing, I remember being placed in my crib for the night. Only one problem, it wasn't dark yet. It was still daylight. Nobody goes to bed when it's still day time, but what did I know? I was almost two years of age. In protest I started shaking my crib, banging against the wall until I could get someone's attention.

Well, it worked. Before I knew it, there was my mother standing at my doorway in her Victoria secrets nightgown. She asked, "What the heck is going on?" Not having the ability to speak, I just stood there, "imprinting" in awe. I could hear my heart going ZOOPA- ZOOPA- ZOOPA... DING! This is the sound your heart makes when you first realize you are in love.

Although I was speechless, I knew right then and there that I was madly, head over heels in love with this woman. Yep, my father had captured lightning in a bottle and I was just happy to be along for the ride!

Yes, my mother was a looker! Her beauty turned heads all over the world! She cleaned up more glamorous than any movie star of her time. Wherever we were stationed, we always had friends gravitate to our home, a place where they felt loved.

Invariably mother would get ready to go to the beauty shop. First she would dress to the nines and do a glamour shot "make up job" complete with loads of perfume. Then she would make an exit passing all of us. The response was always the same. Our friends mouths would drop wide open as they would exclaim, "your mom is BEAUTIFUL!". Yes, our mom was "the bomb"! We were proud to claim her as our own.

My next memory, I was around 3 years old, getting ready of Mass. As a side note, we had recently acquired a puppy dog from hell. Most Weimaraner puppies teeth on shoes and furniture legs. Not this pooch! This pup chose to teeth on our feet and ankles.

In preparation for Mass, Mother was dressing me in a shirt with so much starch, it could stand by itself. Then come the slacks with a 12 inch inseam and matching jacket. The bow tie was the coup d'etat as it seemed to cut off the blood flow to my face. Then she said, "Now go put on your socks and shoes."

This was her first mistake. I wandered into the patio where our puppy spent most of its time doing what puppies do best. I remember stepping into something that felt warm and squishy. I looked down at my feet and saw doggy dooky oozing through my toes. Next I remember hearing my mother shrieking as she scooped me up, at arm's length and whisked me into the kitchen. Wherein she stuck my feet under hot water and soap. Sometimes, the patience of a mother is tried and tested. Eeasch!...

"EJECT, EJECT IMMEDIATELY!"

Now here we are at Mass, in a French cathedral probably 600 years old. The thick scent of musk and mold accentuated its antiquity. Arched stained glass windows as high as the rafters and buttresses surrounded us.

Those mesmerizing- kaleidoscopes had my eyes transfixed onto the brilliant alluring display of colors. I'm sure that all the "stations of the cross" along with congregation of all the saints were represented.

The cathedral interior was rather dimly lit. The sunlight from the east cast an array against the incense smoke. It was like a laser show from Heaven. Celestial sunbeams shone down on the pews.

After about an hour, I start to get fidgety. Remember, I'm 3, full of testosterone and puppy dog tails. My mother looked down at me and very sternly asked, "Can't you sit still for just two hours?" I'm thinking, "No!... No I can't!" I feel like I'm in a body cast with a bow tie that was strangling me.

In those days, Catholic Mass was entirely in Latin and two hours long. Plus everyone around us is poly vooing in Francais. Our mother used logic and reasoning, sometimes to no avail.

So here we are now, Chateaux air force base, France. We are now a family of six as Frenchman, Michael has made his entry into our world. There is an urgent phone call for the fighter pilot's wife. I hear panic in her voice. My next recollection, we are all in our Peugeot SUV, speeding to the flight surgeon's office. I remember mother scolding the fighter pilot for not bailing out soon enough. " l will be damned if I'm going to raise these four kids by myself!".

Apparently Lt. Fighter pilot was coming in for a landing in his F-100 Saber fighter jet over Tripoli in northern Africa. His commanding officer was on his six, as he radioed to him, alerting that his tail was in flames.

"Eject, eject immediately!" was transmitted. Flying over a heavily populated metro area, Tripoli, Libya, Lt. Fighter pilot instinctively banked hard left towards the Mediterranean Sea. Where upon, in a blast he ejected into shark infested waters.

During his cannon blast ejection, a loose buckle had sliced his cheek. His training kicked in as he deployed his mini-raft and shark repellant. After a brief dip, bleeding in the shark infested waters, the fighter pilot was plucked from the cold Mediterranean. His rescue chopper rushed him straight to the flight surgeon for stitches to his cheek.

For the benefit of those unaware of the USAF's aerial arsenal in the mid 1950's, the F-100 Saber was the answer to keeping ahead of the Russian MiG-15. The "cold war" was full on and the F-100 could out maneuver it's adversary and exceed mach 1. This is the speed of sound, in excess of 700 m.p.h.

It was your basic rocket with wings, a tail and ailerons. Aeronautical engineers added a cockpit, throttle, an extremely high caliber machine gun and air to air combat missiles. At this point, Uncle Sam would said, "go get 'em boys, make us proud".

Meanwhile, back at the flight surgeon's office, the fighter pilots wife was giving the young Lieutenant an ear full. "Boy, next time you had better eject and eject immediately! I'll be damned if I'm going to raise these kids by myself!" A timeless sentiment shared by U.S. warrior wives all over this world. A fighter pilot's wife exudes assertiveness which can sometimes be mistaken for selfishness.

After pop's crash and burn, mother adopted a mantra at home, "Boy, you kids had better straighten up and FLY RIGHT or else!". Dad was the fighter pilot. Mother was his wife and our first "female commander in chief".

5

VIGNETTE 3
"CHILDREN, COME HITHER"

It was a relatively nondescript midday. Mother approached my sister and me. "Children, come with me." Okay, I thought. As we followed her down the hallway, I noticed our empress was wearing no clothes. The nap of her long elegant neck graduated into the slope of her slender, statuesque back and "hourglass" waist line.

As she walked, on her toes and the balls of her feet, she seemed to flow with a graceful strut. Her long, legs were well in proportion to her centerfold posterior. Mother walked us into the bathroom, where she sat on the edge of her porcelain throne.

My sister and I stood at her side as she took one of her breasts, tweaking her teat just enough to produce a pearl of mother's milk. "This is how some mother's feed their babies.". I must have missed those sessions, as I most definitely would have remembered that!... She then spread her long, elegant legs to expose the thick black hair of her pelvic girdle. With further instruction to "watch," she then took her long, fair fingers and parted her hair. Exposing glistening pink folds of flesh and skin. I recall thinking that "this was different from what I had.".

As she had a captive audience she announced that, "this was her..." and then there was a long, pregnant pause. She straightened her posture, shoulders back, protruding her breasts, holding her head high. She then flung her beautiful long black hair with a flick of her hand. Breaking the silence, she dismissed us both.

In the absence of any words, my mother's body posture had proclaimed in no uncertain terms, "I am woman, hear me roar!".

The fighter pilot's wife was a perfect baby making machine. She had punched her woman-card with her two first born babies. I felt a sense of transparency and contentment in being one of her first students.

As I waddled back to whatever is that 3 year olds do, I recall feeling the warm and fuzzy embrace of my mother's confidence. I looked forward to a lifetime tutorial and further education.

Not having any other referencing points of view, I knew intrinsically that my mother was the reason that cavemen had chiseled on walls. She was the twinkle in Leonardo's eye and the inspiration for Mona Lisa's smile. The fighter pilot's wife was the Venus de Milo, the Aphrodite of our time.

As the mental fog dissipated, I found ourselves at the Air base maternity infirmary. There was a sense of anticipation as we waited in the car. A young Lieutenant would eventually bring out his wife. As they approached their carriage, mother appeared to be walking very gingerly. Her normally fair complexion was pale and anemic.

Our ride home seemed to last an eternity. There was nay a word spoken. The silence was deafening. An overwhelming sense of melancholy permeated the very air we breathed.

My little heart sank as I realized that there should have been a little bundle of joy in my mother's arms. Inasmuch as children are gifts from God, it was apparent that life offers no guarantees. Any number of biological circumstances can alter the development of life.

The gift of life is a miracle given by the Grace of God, totally void of any assurances. The Fighter pilot's family had had a teeny, tiny angel taken away from their pride and then given up to heaven.

VIGNETTE 4
"HASTA LA VISTA BABY"

Having settled down into new French Chateau quarters, our new home was not complete. At least not until we had hired a local maid to assist the fighter pilots wife. For a young mother in a foreign country, hiring a helping hand was essential as well as affordable. A young, very pretty and adolescent Juanita joined our family. I recall that she was a rather hard worker, always sweeping, mopping and cleaning something.

On one evening, she had gotten a splinter from sweeping. My father offered to help and came to her aid with a pair of tweezers. In order to get the splinter out, he had to stand very close to her. My sister and I were making smooching noises and giggling that daddy was wooing Juanita. I didn't see it at the time, but my mothers' radar was full on.

Little did we know, this would be the last time we would see Juanita. Although it was an obvious "no call", no foul and no harm done," we had signed poor Juanita's walking papers. My mother was extremely pragmatic. Why place fresh meat in front of a pit bull?

Our next maid was easily 50 years Juanita's senior and with half the looks of Mrs. Doubtfire. Whatever she had lacked in looks, she more than compensated with the heart of a loving grandmother. Elsa Doubtfire was to be our nanny for the next couple of years.

On one occasion she invited us to her French country farm for a

Sunday brunch. Next thing I know, we are on a train ride, whirling through a French countryside, "clickety-clack, clickety-clack!". Multiple shades of green continually flying by. Up against a radiant, baby blue sky whisked the beautiful French countryside.

Not having any concept of time, before I knew it, we were running around chasing chickens, piglets and bunny rabbits. The fragrance of freshly cut hay emanating from the barn. The smell of horse and cow manure stuck in our little nostrils.

Monsieur Doubtfire invited my sister, Betty and myself, Bernard into the barn. There against the wall were rows and stacks of chicken-wire cages that seemed to extend to the ceiling. Each compartment housed a cute little bunny. Monsieur told us to pick out our favorite. What did we know? We were three and four respectively.

Next recall was at a beautifully set dinner table with a French smorgasbord of cheeses, fruits, breads and hors d'oeuvres. In comes the main course on a covered silver platter. Our little hearts sank when Elsie uncovered a beautiful, oven browned rabbit. Sautéed in wine, mushrooms, onions, potatoes, carrots and with all the trimmings, "MMmmm, good bunny!".

This was Elsa's way of paying homage to the fighter pilot and his family. After nearly three years of grandmotherly pampering, she had come to the train station to bid us farewell, back to the USA. I remember the lump in my throat as she waved au revoir, until we meet again. Her white hankie waving as she openly sobbed, sobbing as if we were her own… We were…

This was to become a reoccuring prelude to many future departures ahead of us. Every two or three years we were either saying goodbye or making new friends. We were to become experts at enrolling mid-semester for school.

Living a peripatetic existence was a small price to pay for keeping our constitutional republic free from communism. Who could guess what was in store for the fighter pilot, his wife and four cadets?

In retrospection, I realized that the grass is not always greener on the other side of the fence. Many people live their lives amidst a plethora of natural splendors, never taking the time to smell the roses. They scurry around their frantic lives going from point A to point B. Meanwhile, they are totally oblivious to the grandeur at hand.

Carpe diem, inhale the present with all of your senses! Then exhale with exuberant appreciation for the magic of all places unknown.

Absorb the magnificence of the snow-covered Swiss Alps, as they are juxtaposed into a powder blue sky. The snowy, white brilliance brings your eyes to tears. The shimmering of the reflecting sun makes you squint. The blinding light is too much to bear.

Startle in amazement at the symphonic effervescence of the northern lights. Gaze in awe, at the luminescence of yellowish green, as they translucently dance across the subzero night sky. Appreciate the architectural genius of Sir Eiffel's tower on a brilliant Sunday morning.

As we walk on Roman B.C., cobblestoned roads, the alluring fragrance of freshly baked French bread titillates our salivary glands. Excite with exuberance as you try to embrace the warmth of a five foot loaf of french bread, especially when you are only knee high to a grasshopper.

Seize the moment as you drive over a rolling Italian countryside. There in the green distance is the minuscule shimmering light of ancient stained glass. As we draw closer, the tiny reflections escalate.

Suddenly we are dwarfed by a towering fifteenth century Roman Catholic Cathedral. Walking through medieval gravesites one has to stop and reflect at the absolute beauty of such an eloquent display of antiquity.

One can almost hear the clanging of a noble's armor. "To arms, to arms!!!" was the call. In the midst of this medieval essence, one had cause to pause. There in the radiant sunlight laid a series of parallel, rectangular gravesites. Each one filled to the rim with glimmering multi colored gems.

The first is over following with deep ruby reds, followed by dark emerald greens, then by brilliant golden topaz. There are sparkling blue sapphires and white dazzling diamonds as well. These multiple gravesights, vividly encompassed, every hue of the color spectrum.

Moreover, they are refracting a magnanimous array of light. "Wow, these people must have been RICH!". Our bubble burst when the fighter pilot's wife explained that they were simply colored shards of glass. There was nothing simple about any of this...

Living life from the perspective of a USAF fighter pilot is given to enriched and stimulating memories. Living a life without brick and mortar memories is a transient existence filled instead with temporary military housing. We never had the luxury of immersing our roots any deeper than three years. A life without rooted attributes has its drawbacks. Living a life where friendships never exceeding 2 to 3 years, tends to wear heavy on one's heart of hearts.

As a trade off, living life in the present, tends to enhance one's self awareness. Such heightened insight lends to an insatiable desire to inhale with all of one's senses. One tends to absorb with such vivid detail all the memories that encompass a life well lived.

We must surrender ourselves to such rich memories. We simply must exhale and give ourselves up to them. Carpe diem… "seize the moment!".

VIGNETTE 5
"WHERE'S BUNNY?!!!"

At 3 ½ there are only a few things in life to be of any concern. As long as I had a full tummy, a roof over my head and a warm bunny at night, all was right with my world.

Bunny was my security blanket. I had probably received him with an Easter basket the previous year. He was grey and white and oh so warm, soft and cuddly. Bunny was tattered around the edges from the wear of being cuddled and drewled upon nightly. He put me at ease and to sleep each and every night. Bunny was a constant comfort and reliable companion. Linus dragged around his security blanket, I had bunny. He was steadfast and dependable, always there to lull and comfort me to slumberland.

One day, he suddenly and oohhh so abruptly, went missing! I searched high and low throughout our home. "How could this be?" He was just here last night! I searched everywhere, all the nooks and crannies!

Panic was beginning to set in. It was starting to get dark and bunny was nowhere to be found! I remember asking mother if she had seen bunny. She simply shrugged. I recall opening up the kitchen cabinet to dig through the trash can. "Where could you be!???" I recall that everywhere I looked, I could see the fighter pilot's wife watching me,... watching through the corner of her eye.

Bunny was gone!!! He had to have been taken!!! Who would do such a dastardly deed!? I cried myself to sleep, night after night after night… For the rest of my life, I would caudle my pillow as if it were bunny. There was no substitute for my loss. Eventually I found myself in a fetal position and would rock myself to sleep, back and forth, back and forth…

This is a therapeutic behavior pattern designed to intrinsically redistribute the stress hormone, cortisol in our frontal cortex. As a matter of coping with stress, our brains secrete the hormone cortisol. This neurobiologic defense mechanism is an auto response to traumatic stress. The absence of this soothing rocking process can result in permanent brain damage and even death. The introduction of this stress hormone into my young life would prove to be a prelude of detrimental health consequences to come…

When an infant cries out, normally a mother picks her child up and rocks baby back and forth, back and forth. This motion soothes and redistributes the anti stress brain chemical, cortisol to insure healthy brain development.

My rocking, back and forth was my beginning into the journey of neurosis… a behavioral mechanism attributed to PTSD. A life with unresolved suffering and an innate effort to cope with stress.

Forty years later, I asked mother if she had discarded bunny to the dumpster. Instead of saying that she did not remember, she simply replied, "No…" The jury would be out for many years to come.

In retrospection, I never ever remembered my mother giving any of us a scintilla of affection. Her child management style could best be described as "a benevolent dictator", minus the benevolence. There was never an " I love you" or even a hug or a kiss. All of our affection and love came from the fighter pilot, who we all grew to love and pine for… a prelude of things to come! Thank God for the love of our father!

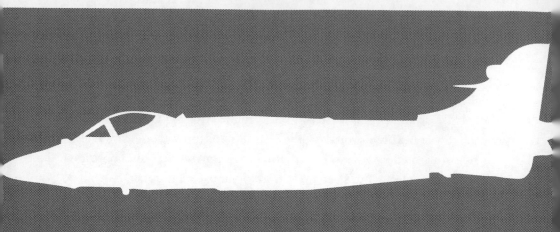

VIGNETTE 6

THE CORP! THE CORP! THE CORP!!!

Next stop, the corp at one of our nation's leading military academies. 1960, home of the fighter pilots alma mater. Lt. Fighter pilot was to take graduate studies to make him a more proficient, highly trained professional killer.

Somewhere in this two year period, my little sisters Anna and Suzy join the ranks of this elite force. We are now a force of eight, the fighter pilot, his commander in chief and six cadets.

In this microcosm, we witnessed Vice President Nixon go down in flames on a black and white television, then the election of J.F.K. On a more personal note, we experienced our first encounter with the shadowy specter of death.

There was a phone call from Space City U.S.A.. This was the first time I had ever heard my mother's voice crack and weep. She told us to go into our rooms and say a prayer for our grandmother. Grandma Fighter pilot never came out of her anesthesia. She was the embodiment of pure love, sweetness and sugar kisses.

That afternoon, Lt. Fighter pilot came home to his pride, anxious for his daily embraces. As he stood at the doorway, mother spread out her arms to stop us from rushing him. His posture stiffened as he asked, "what's wrong". She replied, "It's your mother". His eyes and heart sank. It was a difficult concept for any 1,2,3, 4,5 and 6 year olds to grasp. Seeing my father in a prolonged state of melancholy was heart wrenching. Witnessing him sitting for days with a red eyed thousand yard stare helped to place it into perspective.

Death was something we had heard of on TV or from a third person perspective. Sure, we had seen our hamster die and had flushed several goldfish. There was an unwelcome whisper of gloom on our household. Its presence cast a long, dark shadow, void of any welcome.

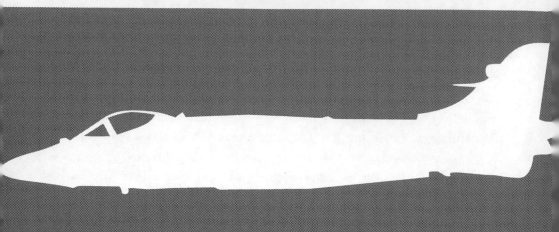

VIGNETTE 7

"SPLISH, SPLASH... WHAM!"

Splish splash went the shallow, warm water in our bathtub. In the absence of bubble bath, my sister and I were bathing together. There we were in crystal clear water, each at opposite ends of the tub, Beatrice, 5 and myself Bernard, 4.

Staring at my genitalia, she asked, "what are those?". Look down at myself, replied, "I don't know…", pulling at my scrotum in innocent self examination. Suddenly I hear the fighter pilot's wife, in a stern voice asking, "What are you doing?!" "Nothing…" I replied. She then asked, "what are those!?" Not knowing what they were, I felt compelled to tell her something. This was the second time in a single moment I had been asked this same question.

Thinking back to how some of my neighborhood buddies had referenced them, I answered, "coconuts?", still looking down at myself in wonderment,

WHAM!!!***#%&@!!!***…

It was a full ganner slap so hard, my little head bounced off the tile wall to my right. Slammed with such intensity that a knot would form on the right side of my head from the sheer impact with a porcelain soap fixture!

As the entire left side of my face and head burned with intensity, I opened my mouth wide to scream in abject horror! To my surprise, nothing would come out! My diaphragm continued to expand, as if I was trying to catch my breath, over and over again... As my diaphram continued to convulse, I began to feel dizzy from lack of air. I heard very faintly,the fighter pilot's wife *screaming* at me, *"Do you want your children to grow up to be idiots?!!"*. Finally I was able to exhale, *"NOOooo!"*. I wailed in utter shock, thankful to be able to breath once more.

The ringing in my left ear was deafening. It would persist in lesser degrees as the days turned into weeks. Eventually the earaches from my ruptured drum would subside, as my hearing would return to near normal.

From this day forward, my emotional DNA, rhetorically speaking, would be scarred for the rest of my life.

My sister was immediately pulled from the tub. I sat there and cried with lessening convulsions, until the water turned cold and my toes began to raisin. This would be the last time we ever bathed together. The rest of my life would be much altered. Having just bathed,... somehow, I still felt dirty.

I learned at a very tender age, that around the *"scorn of a woman"* is drawn a veil, best left undisturbed... On this particular day in my young life, the veil of trust between my mother and myself had been torn. No, fact check that. This is an understatement... It had been ripped to shreds!

Instead of becoming a teaching moment, as I had thought it had been in Europe, I learned to never ever take my eyes off of the fighter pilot's wife's hands. All *trust* in my mother was gone for the rest of my life. I felt distrust and the gradual, dissipation of love in my little heart...

A day or two later, as the family was sitting around watching Walt Disney, I faintly heard my father say to his wife, " you shouldn't have spanked him..." I remember thinking " is that what that was? A spanking???".

In retrospect, it was nothing less than "full on" assault and battery. I had been sucker slapped so HARD... blind-sided! I vowed never, *ever* to be cold cocked again...

In psychotherapeutic terms, this was my *"traumatic life altering event"*. This was ground zero to my trauma. The epicenter and the very beginning of a life much altered… I would not find out for another 50 years that this was the onset to an existence with *severe posttraumatic stress disorder.* For the rest of my life, I would be experiencing chronic symptoms of… PTSD!

From this day forward, I never took my eyes off of the fighter pilot's wife's hands, especially whenever she was within striking distance. This was for self preservation. I constantly found myself *powerless* and at the mercy of her overbearing and persistent will.

At 4 ½, I was a physical mismatch for such an abuse of power. My *sheer will power* would prove to be equal to that of the fighter pilot's wife…

Whenever she would catch me glimpsing at her, she would asked "what the hell are you staring at!? *There was never a right answer…* Then she would reply, "boy, you had better wipe that smirk off your face or I'll knock it off!".

I wasn't even sure what a smirk was, or I would have made every effort to curtail it. She would then come at me with her right arm raised and start striking at my head and shoulders… "I'm going to beat the tar out of you!".

I would immediately bow up, taking a defensive position. I would then raise my right forearm to block a series of several blows. This was a "fight or flight" response and posture. I chose *to stand my ground and fight!*…

Her rules of engagement would change after the first skirmish. I discovered that my defensive posture was causing more pain to her hand than she was inflicting. My elbow and forearm were my only defensive shield against her merciless flurry of strikes.

After breaking a nail and bruising her hand, she would grab the first thing she could find to inflict pain. A yardstick which I usually broke on my first block. She would then become even more agitated, grabbing a wire coat hanger or something more rigid. I can still recall with vivid memory, hearing the wire wisping through the air with each and every strike. Every blocked blow with my forearm would sting with equal intensity.

It mattered not what her weapon of choice was. I had learned to compartmentalize and separate myself from the physical pain. She could have used a lug wrench, I would have refused to whimper… or ever cry!

This infuriated her even more, since it was her goal, to beat me into a whimpering submission. To this end, she would start to verbally attack me. Using semantics such as *"you stupid idiot!"* with each and every blow, over and over and over again. This was to become the order of her day and the repetitive sequence to her behavioral patterns for the next eight to nine long years...

It was apparent that physical abuse was not working, so why not throw in emotional and psychological abuse, just for good measure... over and over and over again.

It would take more than my lifetime to learn to disassociate myself from the emotional pain of these types of inflictions...

As the years went by, I grew numb to the pain and abuse. I found myself dressing for school with long sleeves in warm weather. This, in an effort to hide the embarrassing welts on my forearms.

This embarrassment was a natural reaction to a battery of circumstances over which I had no control or understanding. I must have been guilty as charged, otherwise I wouldn't have been subjected to such severe punishment and vile abuse. This is what all abused children invariably think and feel.

I had learned to give the fighter pilot's wife a wide-berth and tried never to look her in the eye. However, she was always kept in my peripheral line of vision.

For the rest of my life, whenever in her shadow, my "spidey senses" were always full on...

Then there were the times I had to witness her brushing my sisters hair. It's amazing how suppressed memories can come to light when thoughtfully provoked.

I can recall a time when a six year old Betty attempted to escape the reach of the fighter pilot's wife... Seeing that huge acrylic brush in hand, she started to bolt. Her groomer reached out and violently grabbed her by the back of her long, beautiful hair.

Screaming and crying, she was dragged into a submissive kneeling position. She was knelt in front of her, facing away. With that huge pink acrylic brush she would brush their hair with such intensity, huge clumps of hair would accumulate on the brush. Her agitation was compounded and quickly turned to anger as they would not stop crying. "Shut up! Hold still! Stop moving!" I could see the muscles in her jawline tightened up as she clenched and gnashed her teeth.

She was pulling their hair out by the roots!!!

I was incensed as I watched with a disapproving look in my naive little eyes. Somehow, I could sense, that which was unfolding before me was not right… I felt powerless wishing I could help my sister. It was nothing less than extreme *child abuse* on full display…

The fighter pilot's wife noticed me, only to angrily ask once again, "What the hell are you staring at!?" There was never an appropriate response, silence was always my default reaction…

She would then come at me with that huge acrylic brush. The semantics were always the same, "I'm going to beat the tar out of you!!!", WHAM!!!… "I am going to knock that smirk off your face!!!". "You stupid idiot!", BAM!!!… "YOU STUPID IDIOT!!!",POW!!!… Third blow, the intensity of the impact with equal and opposing force from my forearm, snapped that brush right in two.

There was an intense stinging pain. I grimaced with her follow through from that last strike. I grabbed my forearm to stop the bleeding. Her only response was to use the Lord's name in vain against me, followed up with, "you stupid idiot!". Her only concern,… that I had broken her brush. I retreated to the bathroom to self medicate my gashed forearm.

First came the alcohol, to try and stop the bleeding. Then came the iodine and then a good ole bandaid. A suture or two were probably in order but out of the question… This was to become rudimentary procedure to a future lifetime of self medicating ourselves… A lifetime exercise in separation of mind over body, separation from pain…

This would happen a couple of more times. All in an attempt to draw the ire away from my sisters, Betty, #1 and Anna, #5 sibling…

Where was all this pent up anger coming from!?

I wouldn't be able to conjecture for at least another 50 years. The fighter pilot's wife learned not to brush my sister's hair in my presence. They all ended up getting pixie cuts… They all looked so cute!

My younger brothers were not exempt. I recall seeing Felix, #3 chasing Joey, #4 around the house. They were rough housing, as young boys do in exercising their male, alpha traits. The fighter pilot's wife immediately grabbed a belt and went after the both of them.

Realizing they were in the line of fire, they both froze and started screaming bloody murder. All before she ever landed a single blow. She then half heartedly gave each one of them one swat.

I remember thinking, "what a couple of wimps!".

It was then that I realized that she was attempting to beat the male, alpha traits out of me!...

She had literally squashed those male traits in my two younger brothers.

The intentional suppression of one's natural state has profound negative behavioral side effects...

I wasn't around to witness my youngest brother, Kyle's emasculation, #7. Out of 7 siblings, all three of my brothers grew up to be functioning alcoholics. Frankie morphed into a non-functioning alcohol, eventually drinking himself to death... All four of my sisters are socially inclined to partake, some more than others.

My psychiatrist suggests that we are all probably suffering from trauma to one degree or another. She suggests that I should share my diagnosis with my family, "as you are all probably all suffering from PTSD. Initially, I elected not to, as I felt that there was no upside to it... "What are they going to do, throw a pity party for me?!" There was also the fear of being accused of impugning our mother's memory or even ostracism. No thank you!!!...

All the signs of PTSD were all right there on the surface... Felix would rock himself in a fetal position, as I had been. Joey would sit for long periods of time, rubbing his thumb nail back and forth across his upper lip. I tried it myself, to understand what it was he was trying to achieve. To my surprise, it felt soothing,... comforting.

Joey and Kyle would grow up to become angry drunks. For kicks, they were known to go bar hopping with the sole intent of picking fights with other drunks. They were brutal and extremely athletic gladiators, exacting a childhood of pent up and suppressed anger and hostility onto a number of poor unsuspecting souls...

Felix had been doubled dipped in sensitivity and dandelion sauce. His medication of choice was alcohol, as well as THC. He was a hit and a fascination with all the junior high girls, as he was *never* perceived as a penetration threat... All three of my brothers displayed characteristics of the Oedipus complex. They had been infatuated with she who had emasculated them...

Beatrice, the oldest, would grow to be a bitter, extremely angry and combative sibling. She was non-hesitant and quick to use aggressively brutal force to get her way with her underlings.

In retrospect, she was mimicking and parroting our mother. Her anger and abusive nature was always just under the surface. This was a sure sign and symptom of PTSD... Her brutal, slugging tactics ceased on the very day that I slugged her back with equal intensity.

Meeting force with force had solved that bullying situation. One has to wonder how many bullies in our schools are cultivated at home, products stemming from transgenerational violence.

Anti-social behavior is inherently a learned behavior. Our dysfunctional and brutal mentor had made us all insensitive and aloof to one another. The top tier of our dysfunctional dynasty had a tendency of mimicking and parroting our abuser. We were introverted and emotionally stymied. We were all denied any kind of emotional support at any point in our superego's development.

The superego is part of our mind that reflects the social standards learned from our parents in order to gain their acceptance or approval. We were all of us, routine victims of the emotional abandonment and neglect.... We were all us, starving for just a morsel of approval and or affection... As the fighter pilot's wife's first born defiant son, my superego had to contend with the active abandonment of violent physical abuse as well... I had the dubious misfortune of being exposed to both toxins...

Our exposure to the toxicity of emotional neglect breed contemptuous antisocial behavior amongst all of us. To coin a phrase, we were molded into "mean spirited" mini versions of our abuser...

The first four siblings were constantly seeking approval from the fighter pilot's wife. In failing to receive even a modicum of affection, our inner critics would turn to self-hate and self-disgust. Invariably we would turn our frustrations and animosity onto one another. Our ill defined superego's were not equipped with the growth development to understand that our failed attempts at approval were not faults of our own. So we beat ourselves up and eventually one another. Our fledgling superego's were incapable of understanding that the root cause of our dysfunction laid in our parents' shortcomings. The properties of poor parenting breeds a dysfunctional and toxic environment for fledgling egos to grow into healthy superegos...

Throughout her lifetime, Betty exhibited an affinity for vino as well as extreme mood swings, antisocial personality traits with a general air of narcissism, paranoia and reclusiveness, just like our mother... These are all sociopathic traits that would rear their ugly heads throughout a tumultuous childhood..

Anna, #5 and Marie, #8 were seemingly, the only two unscathed offspring... Growing up in emotional chaos, they were prone to keep a low profile and try to assimilate. They grew up to be helpers and healers. The four youngest siblings kerloped into emotional chaos. They all remained socially cautious, always trying to console one another.

The fighter pilot, himself, conjectures that Betty is probably bipolar. I disagreed as she openly exhibited many characteristics of a sociopath. In that particular instance, I could see a retired aviator steeped in blinding denial... If ever, there was a definition for "plausible deniability", he was it!... He had completely delegated our total child mismanagement to his wife...

Looking at my oldest sister, I could see a deeply wounded spirit. She was a victim of child abuse and to large degree... I could very clearly see myself.

Baby Suzy turned out to be a "thumb-sucker", probably from the complete and total lack of motherly nurturing. The fighter pilot's wife was incapable of showing love and with absolutely ZERO affection... At 1½ -2½ years of age, she was physically traumatized with continual abusive slaps to her little hands. To the point she would wail in continuing convulsions until she would literally turn blue, for lack of air... "Mom!, Suzy's turning blue again!!!". Trying my best to comfort and console her, I had to walk away from her. It was all I could do to keep from seeing her pass out for lack of air... All because she wasn't supposed to suck her thumb.

The fighter pilot's wife had turned her anger onto my youngest baby sister. Suzy's adorable, baby hands were placed into mittens and tightly tied. When she chewed through, all types of hot sauces were applied to her thumbs, to no avail. Having been severely traumatised as a baby, she grew up liking habanero tabasco and loving her vino!

Suzy was one of the four younger siblings who remained socially cautious throughout a tumultuous childhood. She remained wide eyed and passive. Always trying to make sense of dysfunction, as we all did. The latter four siblings were more passive-aggressive in nature. The first tier was much more selfish, greedy and aggressive. Betty Lou was the alpa, flat out mean and nasty. A chip off the old block!...

Of eight children, none of the four boys graduated college. Three tried and failed. This, in and of itself, illustrates the ever lasting power of negative expectations… All four sisters graduated or achieved equivalency and at postgraduate levels.

In our household, the absence of male, alpha traits had its advantages…

In hindsight, the fighter pilot's wife's sons were a perfect illustration of negative social engineering… From all of her son's, she had engineered three alcoholics and one defiant, unaccomplished workaholic. I recall in my early 20's telling my parents "I was busy going nowhere in a hurry!...". My father replied that "that was okay, as long as I was doing it to the best of my ability". His wife remained suspiciously quiet...

Keeping painful memories suppressed was crucial in attempting to function as a normal adult, born from child abuse.

It's been said that for every shot of liquor taken, you lose a thousand brain cells. But that's okay because we have billions more to spare! The first ones to die are the sad ones, because everything you say is really funny. The next ones to go are the stupid ones, cause everything you say is really smart. The next ones to die are the quiet ones, because everything you say is really, really loud! The last ones to die are the memory cells… Now these are tough "sons a bitches " to kill!

Is it any wonder that so many adults, born from child abuse, choose alcohol or drugs to try and suppress their trauma? The more they try to destroy those traumatic memories, the stronger they get! THEY JUST WON'T DIE!!!

They're like, like…. "GODZILLA"! The more we try to destroy them, the stronger they become!... These negative memories remain with us a lifetime. The more one medicates the stronger they hold on.

In studying the anatomy and functions of the human brain, it has been determined that the frontal cortex of our brain is where our cognitive thought processes originate.

The summarization of knowledge and understanding is what places us at the top of the food chain…

On the frontal edge of this region is the limbic system. This is where all of our emotions are stored. It is within these regions of our brain that two minute sub-organs dwell. They are known as our hippocampus. They are each just above the ear, about 1 ½ inches into our brain. Our brain is symmetrical by design. They are thought to be the center of emotion, memory and the autonomic nervous system.

Neurobiologists have determined that therein is where our short term and long term memories are processed and stored. Herein, lay all the negative tapes which we carry for the rest of our lives… When will they ever die?

I asked my therapist, many months into my sessions, if they ever die. She replied that she has read somewhere that they die 15 minutes after we do…

I rebutted, " Then why the hell am I here?!" What is the end game?!". She smiled and admitted she had made an attempt at humor. I failed to see her twist in irony as funny…

Truth be told, these ingrained negative memories NEVER go away. *The trick is to soldier on through life, not minding that they are painful… The trick is to simply, not mind that they hurt… much easier said than done!…*

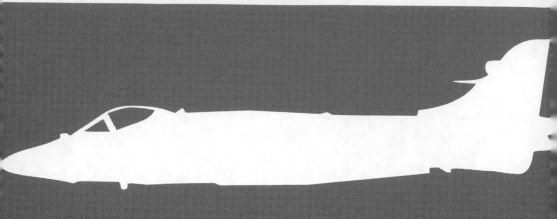

VIGNETTE 8

"THE WALKING-DEAD/ ADULT CHILDREN..."

On any given year, the USA logs 7.4 million child abuse cases. Only God knows how many go unreported! Fact check: 90% of all abused kids never say a word. This means that there are an additional 66.6 million abused kids each and every year that go untold... We survive and endure excruciating, indescribable acts of violence and are incapable of asking for help...

Abused children are too young and innocent in the ways of the world to know what is socially normal. We live our lives in silent anguish... We are oblivious to any standard of social acceptance or permissible level of corporal punishment. At such a tender age, traumatized kids are incapable of framing their abuse with any type of logic or reasoning... We are too naive to discern the difference between discipline, punishment and abuse... So we simply zip it up and lock it away... Silence is in *NO way* bliss. Our norm is to exist in a perverted version of normalcy.

According to the "society for the prevention of cruelty to children", 4-7 children DIE every single day from child abuse, rather 1,460 to 2,555 kids are murdered annually.

In the past 10 years, we have lost less than 7,000 soldiers in both Iraq and Afghanistan. In that same time period we have *MURDERED* more than 25,000 of our kids! All of those 25,000 kids were collateral damage in the war against our own babies… *A SILENT war* that we are all desperately losing!…

In failing to withhold judgement, one has to ask,…

"Is God out to lunch or what!?"…

70% of these child casualties are innocent, helpless babies, 3 or younger. 74.6% of that 70% had died from neglect, possibly from lack of cortisol redistribution or worse. Silence seals their fate and doom… Neglect and secrecy commends their "death sentences"…

Those that survive are merely *reticent reflections of children,* destined to wander through their entire lives with open, gaping emotional wounds. *We grow up to be known in psychotherapeutic terms as "Adult-children".*

So, potentially, every generation, there could be as many as 74 million or more of us, the "walking wounded"! 50% grow up with a warped sense of reality and reward assessment. In perpetuating the abusive cycle, they develop *BAD PICKERS,* as they always choose an abusive spouse. Many of whom are addicted to alcohol and or drugs. Childhood trauma lends a propensity towards self medication… Numbing our senses provides only temporary relief…

This tendency, in and of itself, perpetuates the abusive behavioral pattern to the next generation. Herein lays the continuing legacy. Child abuse crashes through, yet another generational barrier. This transgenerational disease continues to fulfill the self perpetuating cycle of "learned behavior". Fumbling through life, one day at a time, trying to make sense of a series of behavior patterns. Always leaving us wondering… "Why!?"

Why do I continually do things that make my life circumstances worse?! We are constantly navigating through a foggy haze, praying for moments of clarity, hoping that the anger and pain of our inner child will subside. No matter how much we medicate, the symptoms persist! There isn't a chemical known to man that can wash off the toxicity of child torture…

We are the "walking dead", adult-children. Our hearts are severely wounded and numb to the underlying pain. Undiagnosed, it's too deeply buried in our psyches to come to terms. Suppression becomes our most reliable ally. Burying trauma in our psyches is paramount to trying to exist as functioning adult-children.

We are subconsciously being manipulated by negative reinforcement burned into our hippocampi. 20% of the general population are walking wounded, abused as children. We are, all of us "the walking-dead"!

We're like zombies, in search for that single, solitary ray of enlightenment. Somehow we manage to get out of bed every morning, mustering the courage to put one foot in front of the other. Searching for that simple impulse of delight or acceptance. We forge forward, continuing to fumble through our lives.

Some of these poor souls are so tormented, in order to establish a sense of being, they actually *CUT* themselves. All, in an effort to feel the pain of validation.

These walking wounded are known therapeutically as "cutters". I know this personally as my last relationship was with a woman with "borderline syndrome".

In the movie "Fatal Attraction", Glenn Close was a perfect personification of this mental illness. This movie scared the dookie out of everyman in American!

Yet another example of our cortex, separating from our limbic system. We were endowed by our Maker with a psychosomatic defense mechanism. In experiencing traumatic stress, our frontal cortex (brain), subconsciously separates from it's outer edge, our limbic system. Again, this is where all of our memories and emotions dwell.

In extreme cases of abuse, our brains actually develop alternate personalities. They are known to have, "dissociative identity disorders". Split personalities were labeled as politically insensitive. Multiple personas allow them to cope with a horribly brutal childhood.

It is known that "Sybil" had as many as 16 alternate egos, with their genesis from extremely violent, sexual childhood assaults... Child abuse is a key contributor to a variety of mental illnesses... From sea to shining sea, child abuse is practically a national pastime! As you gaze into a crowd of Americans, know that one in every four or five of us have survival toxic and abusive childhoods...

Our limbic system of our cortex has billions of neurotransmitters and receivers. They electro-chemically, somehow know to cut off the "traumatic memories, the bad stuff" to our conscious thought processes. As a survival and defensive mode, extreme trauma causes the complete dissociation of mind and body.

Please excuse the psychological minutiae, as it is necessary in understanding how our brains are wired and cope with the extreme stress of mental trauma.

This Psychological chaos is the perfect breeding ground for a slew of mental illness disorders...

"Cutters", these poor souls are so desperate for any kind of validation, so much so that they actually draw own blood to achieve it. They neurotically slash their wrists, arms or legs. All for just a whispered sensation of self validation,... anything to prove to themselves that they exist! "I can feel pain and I can see blood, therefore I am!"...

Enduring a childhood of violent and oftentimes sexual abuse, followed up with an insurmountable amount of neglect... deeply scars the human psyche! Abuse leaves a deeply disturbed void in our existence. It screams out in utter anguish, demanding an explanation... Human nature abhors a vacuum!

Pain is the assurance of their existence... it fills their void...

Is it any wonder we have so many psychopaths running around mass murdering our children. Since Columbine, there have been 10 educational mass shootings where 5 or more deaths were recorded. The body count is at 128, all innocent babes, lost at the hands of deeply disturbed and deranged souls.

In our most recent academic, mass murder attempt, again near Columbine, luckily only one brave soul was murdered. He gave his life, subduing a Trump hating, mentally deranged, 16 year old transexual...

Initially it was reported that one of the shooters was historically our first female assailant. A definite "Breaking News" pulitzer headliner!... He was a young woman, born in a boy's body... As soon as the media reported that the assailant was a protected class member of the LBGTQ community, the story was quickly buried... His/her... their final social media tweet was, "Fuck society!"...

When will our schools ever be safe again!?

It is my contention that authorities, media and politicians in this society, downplay the mental health issue. That which they can not relate to or understand, scares them. They nonchalantly dismiss the "mental illness issue as if they were in a low stakes poker game. They play it like a trump card. Once they play lip service to the "mental illness" factor, they conveniently sweep it under the carpet…

What they don't realize is that they are ALL playing a HIGH STAKES gamble. Failure to do anything is *an open invitation for the mentally deranged.* Our children's lives and well being are being "annied up"!

VIGNETTE 9

THE STIGMA OF MENTAL ILLNESS...

Truth and Consequences...

There is an extremely negative, social stigma that rears its *ugly head* whenever "mental illness" is brought up. People's body language tell the story. Arms are crossed while body positions push back, as if it were contagious. Ignorance and fear of the subject, clouds the clarity of our vision. We fail to see the severe magnitude of this dilemma.

Stress from traumatic, childhood experiences can poison the human mind. You don't have to have toured Iraq to suffer from PTSD...

God bless our patriots!... We are losing 22 vets every day from suicide and unresolved suffering stemming from PTSD. The negative stigma of seeking therapy can seal their fate... Therapy is in no way a cure all for these traumatized patriots. The specter of depression is seeping in and snatching the life right out of them... The human mind was not meant to witness and readily process the carnage of war...

By that same token, violent child abuse is equally difficult to mentally process... It's important to note that PTSD can be born from extreme neglect, constant physical and verbal bashings in and of themselves...

31

Traumatic assaults from words alone can be just as devastating as the trauma induced be physical violations... Aggressive and passive abandonment, rather abuse, both physical and verbal exacts an insurmountable degree of pain and anguish on our fledgling minds. The simultaneous enactment of verbal and physical "weapons of mental destruction" presents a double entendre to our superegos… Physical wounds will heal. Negative semantics cut to the very core of our existence, leaving a gapping, throbbing wound that can never be forgotten… To this I can personally attest!...

The sheer numbers of non-reported child abuse cases *every year* exceeds 73 million. These poor souls are unreported, collaterally damaged… It's an *UNSPOKEN,* silent war, repeated generation after generation. When will it ever stop?! To even ask this question, in and of itself is *UNSPEAKABLE!*

You don't have to be a rocket scientist to figure out that we are heading "full throttle" into the "perfect psychosomatic storm.". We are a society that harbors a pervasive, deep and dark, unspeakable *transgenerational tendency.* Year after year, we generate more than 73,500,000 abused children, *MURDERING* between 1,460 and 2,500 of our own kids!... *MURDERING, … MURDERING,… MURDERING,… MURDERING,… MURDERING,… MURDERING,… MURDERING,… MURDE RING,… MURDERING,… MURDERING,… MURDERING,… MURDERING,… MURDERING,… MURDERING,… MURDERING,… MURDERING,… MURDE RING,… MURDERING,… MURDERING,… MURDERING,… MURDERING,… MURDERING,… MURDE RING,…MURDERING,… MURDERING,…*

our own
kids..
Therein lies the silent minority who were literally dying to be heard!...

We never speak a word of our personal hell... Those that survive, all grow up to be "adult children".

We are potentially cultivating hundreds of thousands of psychopaths! No… fact check that. Statistically speaking, every generation 1% of our population are psychopaths! Over 3,6 million psychopaths with an additional 3-5%, 10-18 million sociopaths at any given time are wandering amongst the "the walking wounded".

They are all innocuous, *SEEMINGLY HARMLESS*. This is merely a facade, as they are potentially malevolent, incapable of feeling any remorse... They cloak themselves in mediocracy then blend into our society.

By definition, psychopaths and sociopaths are considered to be inflicted with antisocial personality disorders. All of whom share several characteristics as common denominators. They are;

- selfish and reclusive introverts, silent and unspoken, socially nervous and self- conscious, most comfortable alone and within a familiar surrounding.
- more times than not, inordinately selfish narcissists with inflated senses of self-worth.
- All are numb from the neck up as they are completely separated from their limbic systems, as they are *incapable of feeling any emotions.*
- Superficially charming.
- pathological liars that con and manipulate others.
- callousness, unable to be empathetic but with an extreme ability to remain focused. Incapable of expressing love or affection.
- They are capable of mimicking emotions yet incapable of truly expressing them. They are experts at feigning all spectrums of human emotion. Like chameleons, they use their talents as cloaking and grooming devices to control and manipulate others.

Many high functioning psychopaths possess an extremely high I.Q. It is theorized that a percentage of the antisocial personality impaired are born predisposed with this neurological propensity and dopamine hormonal imbalance. Trauma induced by extreme child abuse claims the lions share of this segment of our population.

It is important to note that not all psychopaths are potentially bad. Many use their psychological traits and flourish as CEOs, captains of industry and leaders of governments. Their ability to be unencumbered with human emotion allows them to remain laser focused and goal orientated. Antisocial personality disorders have their social upside.

While on the downside, others possess a frontal cerebrum which has been violently separated from their limbic portion of their cortex. These poor souls were victims of extreme torture as children, while some of whom suffer from an excessive amount of the hormone, dopamine or faulty cerebral wiring.

Dopamine, a "feel good" hormone associates us with feelings of euphoria, bliss, motivation and concentration. It acts as a brain chemical called a neurotransmitter, interacting with a hundred billion other neuro-receivers. All those electrochemical neurons are charging throughout our cerebral matrix.

These inflicted souls blend into our society without a hint of malevolence. Like time bombs, tick, tick, ticking away. When and where ever they explode,… nobody can ever know.

Our *Texas Lt. governor, Dan Patrick* is the ONLY politician to *EVER* put his money where his mouth is. He donated, out of pocket, metal detectors to Santa Fe high school. This in response to the Santa Fe's mass execution of 10 of our children and teachers. I still grieve for our children and the families at Virginia Tech, Columbine, Sandy Hook (elementary) and Parkland High schools...

Instead of receiving positive accolades, the media/political opposition choose to bash him! Accusations of political grandstanding!? *WHAT!?*... This is the first time a politician tries to help and curtail the mass murder of our children.

He is chastised?!!!

This exhibition of such *"hateful partisanship"* exposes a murky dimension to a very serious underlying problem,...

NAKED POLITICAL INSANITY!!!...

Herein lays the *TRUE* mental disorder!!! *Extreme "hateful partisanship" is the real mental disorder!...*

Lt. Governor Dan's sincere gesture is to help save our kids. It is as

PURE a gesture of love as you will ever find!… It's unfortunate that we have to harden our schools to avert yet another incident of mass murder. It's worked in Israel.

Lt. Governor Dan's sole intent was to console Santa Fe's community, to enhance our children's safety. All of these communities are suffering from PTSD. They all need and deserve our love, help and consoling.

Instead of *doing what is right for the right reason*, politicians treat the lives and well being of our children like a political football. They are all playing "Russian roulette" with our children's lives and well being. Oh my GOD!!!

THE RUSSIANS! THE RUSSIANS! THE RUSSIANS!…

"Let's just punt the ball down the field…", then we can relax with the knowledge that our reelaction coffiours remain full. As long as we may continue our insider trading. As long as we get to keep that" hourde", and then retire a Go-zillionaire,… all will be right in our world. Let us keep this "gravy train" on the tracks, "Why rock the boat? Why hurt my chances for reelection?". "I have to go along to get along"…

Therein lays the perceived mindset in D.C., on both sides of the aisle.

95% of all political incumbents get re-elected… many of whom become "lifers", leaving office, only when recalled by death… They come into service with modest financial portfolios and leave as multi-millionaires hundreds of times over… Seldom do we ever elect a representative, on either side of the aisle that holds true to "The People"…

unafraid of doing the right thing for the right reason…

Our forefathers never intended that we be led by mealy-mouthed professional politicians;… whose only preoccupation is to get reelected;… whose prelude to every decision is how it will affect my reelection's chances;… who place the greater good of their political survival over the greater good of the country;… who ultimately leave office to peddle their influence in government to the highest bidders… Innocuously, they blend into the established "status quo".

Blessed are the chosen few, those who operate above "political correction". First and foremost, they are selfless human beings. These are the TRUE patriots of the people. They pull from their own financial resources to give back to their communities, *turning their backs to personal enrichment.*

These are the *TRUE, FEARLESS* servants. They give freely of themselves. They volunteer their time and treasure. An extreme and select few *FORGO ANY SALARY!*… All for the PURE intent of SERVICE. Trying to make our country great! These states people are TRULY ALIVE! Instead of admonishing them,…

> *their likenesses should be chiseled on to the face of "mount Rushmore!".*

WE HAVE SERIOUS PROBLEMS!!!

Potentially violent psychopaths quietly living amongst us all… They are emotionless zombies, incapable of ANY remorse or feelings.

Herein lays the root of psychopathic mass murderers… *the unspeakable social flaw of transgenerational child abuse!* It simply isn't enough to write off yet another bloodletting as "*just another case of the mentally ill acting out.*"!

These tortured adult-children are neurologically incapable of realizing the consequences of their abhorrent actions.

This, coupled with the infamous worldwide notoriety via the internet, is a formula for the perfect "psychopathic storm". These tortured souls have a total and complete disregard for life.

Must we be forever vigilant? For 27 years, since the mass murder at Luby's in Killeen, Tx., I have been sitting in restaurants, *always facing the front door.* Always poised and ready to pick up a table and charge any gun slinging maniac that might walk in… "Hypervigilance"…

Since Cain, the first human born to mankind, murdered Abel, his brother and the first to die, we are continually made well aware of the atrocious capabilities of man… *Free will!… God's greatest gift… and curse to us all…*

On this particular day in Texas, 27 years ago, the veil of social trust had been completely ripped to shreds!… Myself, along with many millions of Americans had lost all faith in our public safety and social security!…

When will the next "son of Sam" appear and go Berkowitz? When will someone else go "postal" on us?

NEWS FLASH!

May 31, 2019, a dozen city employees murdered, several more gun shot at Virginia Beach. A lifelong public utility worker goes "postal"!… As usual, the media is scurrying to find a motive, as if this insanity can be somehow, someway be justified!… It matters NOT how this sicko-psycho can be humanized by reason! He was a total waste of psycho carbon matter who snatched 12 innocent souls from their loved ones. *They are asking the wrong questions!…*

There is a glaring reason for this systemic societal flaw.. If only we had the courage to admit it and face it for what it is… What we should be asking is…

WHEN IF EVER, WILL WE EVER FEEL COMPLETELY SAFE IN PUBLIC AND IN OUR SCHOOL AGAIN?!

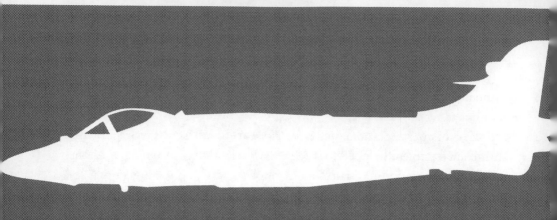

CULTIVATING MENTAL ILLNESS

A systemic, societal cesspool

There are six basic emotions, glad: sad: mad, scared, ashamed and disgusted. When we combine any random two in various pairings, we come up with 156 more. Based on commercial T.V. it would appear that we have a pill for everyone of them...

Our brains are an extremely complex, highly sophisticated central processing units. It's neurobiological, electrochemical characteristics power all of our functions, thoughts, dreams and aspirations.

Our CPU's were designed by our Maker with psychosomatic-safety devices which allow us to survive traumatic events. Their function is to keep us in our "right mind" and to cope with traumatic stress. This, so that we can soldier on, so that we may go onto propagate our species.

Imagine if you would, 10,000 years B.C., a hunter, gatherer has had a bad day trying to kill a woolly mammoth. He can't just go back to his cave and sulk. His family will starve. He must separate himself from the traumatic stress then go onto make that next kill.

36% of our prison population were abused children. 25% of them are male psychopaths... They're the ticking time bombs that have been caught and caged... These are the "Hannibal Lectors" amongst us all. They are innocuous chameleons. They blend in and change their colors to infiltrate our masses. They are the silent and potentially deadly, "walking wounded".

These stealthed manics emerge innocuously from their holes and can spew terror at any given moment. Consider that psychopaths have already disconnected their rational thinking from their ability to process emotions… Psychological sensory overload can stress and strain any remnants left in their sense of reality... Their mental flexibility can only bend to a finite amount of stress,… until something...

SNAPS!!!...

Case in point, 2017, Alexandria, Virginia, near our capital. A registered democratic and confirmed "TRUMP HATING" *psychopath* opens fires on our GOP playing softball. My congressman, Roger Williams, broke his ankle driving into a dugout to avoid the spray of gunfire. "It was like diving into a pool, only without the water!...".

Naked progressive political insanity running amuck!

Just the other day, after nearly a year of investigation, the Las Vegas police reported that *they are unable* to come up with a motive for the worst mass slaughter in American history of histories.

Stereotypically, 58 *christian, conservative,* country western fans are brutally and summarily murdered. *It could be aptly described as a "human turkey shoot"...* Politically biased Nevada authorities claim they were *unable* to determine why these 58 Americans *WERE GUNNED DOWN* with another 851 receiving "bullet hole" trauma. Several hundred more had the abhorrent misfortune of witnessing bystanders heads exploding into a pink mist…

What a farce!!!

As in the silence of the lambs, we are being lead to an uncontested slaughter. *Passive-aggressive political bias, complacency* and *denial* are leading us to our next mass killing field… all "soft targets". It's only a matter of time.

NEWS FLASH!

Jacksonville, Florida, yet another murderous psychopath, a military aged male, opens fire at a gaming convention. He murders 2, wounds and attempts to murder 11 more before administering self justice, killing his own, dead soul.

The progressive media initially reports that he was a Trump supporter, as they often do. As they had falsely I.D.ed as a T.E.A. party member the Aurora, Colorado's mass theatre murderer…

After *social media investigation,* it was disclosed that he was YET another "Trump hater", describing our president's constituents as "Trump tarts!".

Social media has become our most reliable, objective and unbiased reporter since Watergate! *It is a bastion to our first amendment, an OASIS revealing the TRUTH… free of spin…*

It's unbiased, candid nature of self acclamation, makes it impossible for a zebra to hides its stripes…

In our own words, we define in no uncertain terms who we actually are…

So what that social-media, inadvertently reported, just days into the Las Vegas investigation, a *"Freudian sledgehammer"!*

Some reporters accidentally exposed the unvarnished truth, airing a *social media* photo of this sicko psychopath wearing a *"PINK VAGINA"* cap!!! Realizing their political foo-pah, yet another "Trump hater" exposed, the media quickly buried it…

He was grinning ear to ear!… Geah!… What a complete and total waste of carbon matter!!!

Is it any wonder that the media so abruptly and prematurely pulled all coverage to absolutely the most abhorrent mass murder in USA history?! What could this mean?!

CONNECT THE DOTS!

Not that it was necessary, did anybody bother to check his voting records, as was done with that psychopath who tried to mow down our GOP playing ball? Of course not!

This would stain *"extreme political bias"* and tag it to the worst mass slaughter in our history!... We can't have that, now can we?!

That would expose an obvious precept about our political insanity.

So what that Congresswoman Maxine Waters, *a ranking member of the financial services committee*, and the media/political opposition are spewing *PURE VILE HATRED* and lies on a daily basis.

- So what that they are encouraging everyone, politically opposed to them to extreme confrontation! "Get in their faces at a gas station or wherever they may be in public" " If you see them at a restaurant, sitting down for dinner, *RUN THEM OFF!*"
- So what that a renowned Houston restaurant would receive "death threats" for serving our attorney general.
- So what that a relatively unknown actress would exclaim, "Where is John Wilkes Booth when we need him?!".
- So what that a republican congressman is nearly stabbed to death in California.
- So what that "media/political opposition" exhibits effigies of our presidents "decapitated" head on prime time T.V..

They regurgitate, "This is free speech!"... in actuality, it is *FREE...free HATE SPEECH, with total and complete impunity!!!*

Do they actually think that this will NOT have
any *negative consequences?!*

They may as well *"scream FIRE in a movie theatre!!!".* Isn't this free speech as well?!!

With the existence of 3.6 million psychopaths and another 10-18 million sociopaths running around in this country, this *is* inciting mass murder of biblical proportions!

For the love of GOD, accept political defeat and learn to live with disappointment!

We have serious problems! We need sane people and cooler heads to prevail!

If you think I'm being politically biased, you couldn't be further from the truth. Denial is completely blinding us to an obvious point of contingency… which is at the root of many of our social ills… There is a direct cause and effect relationship between…

how we treat our kids and how we treat one another…

That root is toxic child torture!!! The SPCC supplies the cold hard data each and every year! Child abusers murder 1400-2500 of our kids every fucking year!!!… Please do not confuse my passion on this topic as mere vulgarity. My anger exists on several personal levels as I myself was severely abused, physically, psychologically and emotionally for my entire childhood…

If ever there were a subjective topic with the general aire of social avoidance, it is this one!… Tis the nature of man to avoid the discomfort of "Death, pain and suffering.". *Child abuse encompasses all three!…*

In the absence of an informative narrative on such a grim and tabooed topic, I am attempting to address it "head on"!… Sometimes we must face down our deepest, darkest most appalling secrets to achieve absolution… Guilt and the shameful memories of aggressive and anguished punishment are as insurmountable a yoke to bear as anyone could conceive…

This brings to my mind an inspiring quote from the late "Pulitzer Prize" winner for literature", Toni Morrison. "If there is a book that you want to read, but it hasn't been written yet, you must be the one to write it."…

Perhaps no one wants to read about the 70-80 million transgenerationally tortured Americans that are born of toxically anguished childhoods... or perhaps they would... This social disease makes no distinction between sex, race, creed or social status!... Finally a narrative about "abused kids", written by an "abused child"...

At the inception of the Roman dynasty, the emperor Caligula-Gaius Julias Cesar marked the beginning to the moral decay of the empire, 37-24 A.D. His reign is personified for its cruelty, sadism, extravagance and sexual perversions... Caligula's sick sadistic sexual appetite and drunken debauchery proceeds his death as his insanity lives on in the annals of history. He was known for his drunken, gluttonous, whore infested parties. His sanctuary was overlooking a beautiful Roman cliff.

For dessert and his amusement, his excellency would take in and rape his loyal subjects infant babies from every orifice possible. Then, in a drunken stooper he would drop kick them off of the cliff to their deaths, laughing hysterically as their brains were dashed out against the rocks below!...

This marked the beginning of the end for this once great empire. The absolute and total moral decay of this society began to devore Rome from the inside out. Like a voracious "flesh eating bacteria", Rome would succumb to its moral decay... This once great Republic imploded for all of history to see.

This once great Roman Repuplican legislature had been purchased by their emperor in exchange for his unconstrained personal power. Lobbying and countervailing for power and influence with taxpayer's riches knows no time table. It appears that we haven't learned from our past...

At Rome's core of destruction was the complete and total disregard for our children's lives!!! The sanctity of life had been cheapened and thrown to the Roman cobble stoned curb... Deja vu???

Most recently, in this great Republic of ours, one of our oldest and greatest legislatures, historically founded by the Dutch as "New Amsterdam", passed a resolution giving it's citizens the right to MURDER babies after they have been born!!! Upon making that proclamation, they ENTIRE elected assembly came to their feet with a "STANDING OVATION"!!!

Caligula smiles from HELL!!!...

Has history taught us nothing?! Why not simply drop kick our unwanted babies off of a cliff???

Our Republic will go the way of our children...

From this social malignancy is spawned the entire gamut of mental illnesses which begets psychopathic mass murderers. This social cancer metastasizes to every level of our society. If this, in and of itself does not alarm you?...

YOUR REFUSING TO SEE THE 800 POUND PINK ELEPHANT IN THE ROOM!...

Current political events coupled with the pulse of an irate media is stirring up a lethal concoction... Before we continue drinking this deadly kool-aid, it is absolutely imperative that we read the writing on the wall! We are way overdue for a major social revelation...

We all need to wake up and smell the coffee...

Extreme political ideology, on both sides of the aisle has poisoned our ability to communicate, let alone compromise. Extreme political indifference is fueling and fanning the flames of complete and utter madness. Gone are the days, as Americans, that we can simply agree to disagree... and coexist.

Until we realize we are adding fauter for the mentally deranged, we will continue to be in for rude awakenings,... day, after day, after day!

When will the next shoe drop???

July 28, 2019, Gilroy in northern California. Yet another mentally deranged 19 year old male, exclaims how "angry" he is before he starts mowing down innocence... Rapid fire anger is an underlying symptom of PTSD with its genesis in child abuse. Mental illness "guns down" the silence of the lambs... Three murdered, including a six year old little boy and a 12 year old little girl. 15 more wounded before police administer justice and take him out...

August 3, 2019 yet another mass murder spree in El Paso, Texas. Another angry 21 year old male assassin opens up at an extremely busy Walmart, murdering 22 innocent unsuspecting souls. 26 others were critically wounded, including a 4 month old baby.

Just 13 hours earlier, on this very same day 9 more murdered in Dayton, Ohio!!! This is America's first double header mass murder... A dubious distinction to say the least. Gilroy, California would make it a trifecta...

Sept. 1, 2019, Odessa, Texas, almost a month after this horrendous trifecta, 7 more murdered by mental illness!... 22 more innocent bystanders receive wounds in the latest maniacal rampage. Our latest forecast is perpetually grim to mostly deadly...

As usual, there are those screaming gun control, blaming everybody that subscribes to the second amendment. A number of political light weights are clamoring at the top of their lungs to confiscate our guns. What they should all be screaming is...

WHEN WHERE AND WHY do we continue to cultivate maniacal malcontents?

PTSD born from child abuse is manufacturing 70-80 million abused adult children each and every generation, 3.6 million psychopaths and another 18 million sociopaths. FBI statistics show that 27% of all mass murderers are cold calculated planners, two years in the making. Another 25% are simply spontaneous psychopaths who succumb to sensory overload. WHATEVER THEIR MOTIVATIONS are, they all possess one common denominator... raging PTSD anger.

I fully realize that my conclusions on such a dark, forboden subject may appear to be a convoluted stretch,

UNLESS YOU HAVE WALKED A MILE IN MY SHOES!!!

Getting inside the mind-set of a tormented soul is more easily infiltrated by one of the same kindred experiences with a tortured toxic childhood as the lowest common denominator.

Since the 1966 Whitman mass shooting in Austin, Texas, a "Blue-ribbon" panel of psychologists had concluded that the common denominator among ALL mass shooters since then have been that they're all products of a dysfunctional and abusive toxic childhood. Duuhhh!...

With the pervasiveness of child torture in our country, it is a mathematical and statistical certainty that this neusiating trend will go on into perpetuity. Before going on his raging rampage, this particular sicko-psychopath stabbed his "mother dearest"to death. He then went on to jibjab his dear wife in the same manner. One has to wonder if he had "mommy issues"... Hmmm... In actuality, his father was an abusive, violent drunk...

We all live in a society which harbors 70-80 million, deeply wounded human-animals every generation... Trauma, anger and varying degrees of extreme rage are a parallel similarity among all of us... At times, we entertain thoughts of enacting severe retribution to fulfill a twisted need for "misplaced" vengeance. More times than not, reason and logic prevents the empowerment of such an extreme emotional irruption "acting out". Our humanity gets in the way of a potential "human time bomb"... The FBI has determined that in 25% of studied psychopathic mass murderers, something...

SNAPS!!!

At which time, these maniacal brains experience a dopamine hormonal rush with a sensational overload equivalent to that of an orgasmic euphoria... Their motivation and concentration is laser focused by this brain chemical. With each act of twisted misguided vengeance, these sicko-psychopaths get off on the carnage that they have inflicted... *For whatever their motives,* their actions are empowered by their sick, self-serving lust for revenge... Ultimately, retribution justifies their unconscionable acts of violence. Thus our genocidal tendencies continue to no avail...

Invariably, *child abuse crashes,* violently through every generational barrier. We have created the perfect breeding ground for psychotic behavior. It has metastasized itself onto *all time and continuum and all levels of our society.*

From the time that Cain murdered Abel to the time the Menendez brothers murdered their Beverly Hills parents in 1989. The latter set of brothers defensively claiming they were sexually molested and brutally beaten their entire lives to most recently, when 5 year old Andrew Freund was silently beaten to death by his "blue collar" sperm donor... Through time and continuum child abuse and murder have shown no social distinctions...

It appears, *RECENTLY*, that extreme political ideology has permeated the mentally deranged. Long gone is our sanctity for life... *and along with it, our sense of social security.*

If you live in a sanctuary city, there are literally tens of thousands of homeless "walking wounded"! They are all broken souls... An overwhelming majority of them have addictions as well as psychosomatic events in their traumatic past. Who needs to watch "The walking-dead" on TV. We are surrounded everyday by the real deal,... reality TV in real time.

Speaking to social workers at the ARCH, Austin Resource Center for the Homeless, their homeless population varies by the change of seasons and social events. That number ebbs and flows from four thousand to as many as eight to twelve thousand.

During musical events, such as Austin city limits and South by Southwest, the "walking wounded" are bused in from all over the country. As Americans, we're very generous people. 400 thousand tourists from all over the world is a panhandler's dream!

Almost every major highway overpass harbors mini-communities of the walking wounded. They're complete with mattresses, tents and a slew of shopping carts. All lined up and filled to the rim with all their worldly possessions. It tears my heart to see a homeless young lady, pregnant with child!

Just yesterday, as I was driving under an overpass. There in the shade of 110 degree heat index laid a lost adult-child, slumbered with his beautiful white pitbull puppy. Thank God for the unconditional love of our poochies.

I stopped with flashers on to honk and offer him money. He was too deep into medicated REM sleep to respond. His puppy raised a sleepy head then settled back down. That pup was probably thinking, "this is the longest walk we've ever been on. Daddy, when are we going home"... I drove on with a heavy heart...

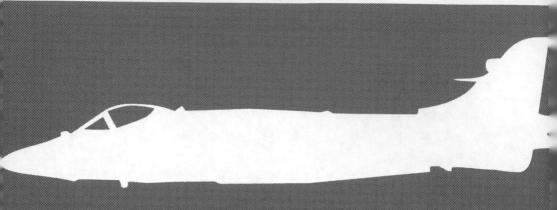

SEVERING THE TOXIC HEAD OF TRANSGENERATIONAL CHILD ABUSE!

Inasmuch as I have survived a tumultuous and brutal childhood, I am in no way attempting to establish blame or judgement on anybody... This is a concerted attempt to shine a blinding spotlight onto the "truth and consequences" of such deep, dark, foreboding social tendency. If only we had the courage and strength of character to see it for what it is...

In failing to withhold love from the victims of this social pariah, wouldn't I be remiss in not offering up just one possible solution to this societal travesty?

- *Fact:* We are reporting 7.4 million child abuse cases each and every year. There is another silent 90% or 66.6 million "wounded souls" produced *every generation*. These are our muted, anguished babes, living in silent misery... Furthermore, we have silently *murdered* 1500 to 2500 of these innocent children on an annual basis. Somehow, the words "child-abuse" just doesn't seem to adequately encapsulate this horror. *For the love of GOD, where is the outcry?! Why not # this!?*

- *Fact:* Our general population is harboring an innocuous 1% or 3.6 million psychopaths. Another 3-5% of our general population are sociopaths, rather another 10-18 million embittered, delusional souls, void of conscience. They attempt to innocuously blend in. These are the potential "Hannibal Lector's" silently living amongst us all. As ticking time bombs, no one ever knows when they will unleash their welded up anguish and anger…

- *Fact:* We live in a society torn apart by political indifference and the *insanity of extreme political partisanship!* This, coupled with the polarizing efforts of a majority of the media/political opposition, invariably throwing gasoline into the flames of extreme indifference. *Political extremism* is inciting psychopathic acts of aggression… i.e.; Alexandria, Virginia, where a sicko-psycho tried to mow down our GOP at play. Lest we forget the "vagina cap wearing" psycho in Las Vegas, wherein 58 innocents were murdered, leaving 851 more with gunshot trauma. August 3, 2019, 20 more murdered and 26 wounded in El Paso, Texas… preceded by Dayton, Ohio where 9 more we gunned down with 27 suffering gunshot trauma. The infamous list of human atrocities goes on and on… Is it ever ending???

- *Fact:* Since Columbine, we have had 10 mass murders in our educational institutions, claiming 128 of our babies.

In weighing these four, indisputable *stone cold facts*, one does not have to be a brain surgeon to connect the dots. We are heading full throttle into the "perfect psychopathic storm"! No,… check that.

We are there!

Instead of rolling with the punches, how can we risk just one more innocent life?! Why don't we make a concerted, constructive attempt to curtail this genocidal dilemma. Why not attempt to nip this societal pariah in the bud.

First, we need to admit that we have a systemic societal flaw. We are producing the perfect breeding grounds for psychopaths to blossom.

The root of our psychopathic, murderous epidemics, is largely, arguably born from severely abused childhoods. This, coupled with faulty neuro-cortex wiring and incidents of excessive amounts of the hormone, dopamine in some of our brains.

- *Why not* implement an educational component into our educational infrastructures?
- *Why not, proactively* identify and attempt to heal our "walking wounded" at its earliest stages, pre-school and up?
- *Why not* teach our educators to recognize and assess the signs and symptoms of PTSD born from childhood maltreatment.

In every level of our educational institutions, elementary, middle and high schools, *supplement* our P.E. classes with a six week segment on mental health and well being.

We've done this for many generations with sex education. Why not train our P.E. teachers in a "quick study" course on the mental health affects of PTSD stemming from child abuse. Good physical and mental health should be symbiotic. We can't have one without the other. This would initiate our coaches as P.M.E. teachers, physical and mental eductaters.

- <u>Use a simple and elementary, 20 questionnaire, designed by therapists to identify, numerically rate and rank levels of PTSD.</u>
- Once students have been potentially identified and numerically rated, have them spend time with a trained therapist. Schedule them one hour per week, with a designated mental health counsellor. *YES, we need to hire and assign to each and every school in America, one therapist.*
- *Be prepared to notify CPS if necessary. January 24, 2019, in Japan, a 10 year old little girl, Mia Kurihara confided in her teacher through the use of a "child bullying" survey. She let her teachers know that she was being beaten on a daily basis by her father. Instead of calling CPS, they betrayed this baby's plea for help and in defying their promise of*

confidence by telling her parents. Within 24 hours, she was tortured and beaten to death. Her parents were sentenced to 25 years in prison.

- *We must be prepared to read the "Miranda rights" to abusive parents...*
- Have our "walking wounded" read from a self help curriculum, age appropriate, to their academic levels.
- After a predetermined period of sessions, follow up with another 20 questionnaire to monitor their progress.
- Take a proactive and nurturing approach to positively modify our children's behavioral and mental health issues.
- Provide an atmosphere of positive reward and reinforcement towards our kids mental well being. *Let us attempt to destigmatize the negativism of mental illness!!!*

Why not enact these simple and relatively inexpensive "proactive mental health" procedures in every elementary, middle and high schools in America. We just might stem the tide of our *transgenerational tendency of child abuse.*

90% of all abused children are living their lives in silent desperation, "the silent minority". They are scared to death of telling anyone of their deepest, darkest most appalling secrets. They are *ALL* silently screaming out with a decried and anguished voice. Hopelessly, *HELPLESSLY* yearning for a loving hand to be extended. They are literally "dying" to be heard!!!

- *How can we NOT do something to help them all!?*
- *How can we NOT throw them a lifeline?!...*
- *How is it possible, NOT to offer a helping hand!?*

Of course, there will be many politicians claiming that the legal liabilities and the cost of these expenditures are too much to bare!

- *However,* we *can* afford to annually subsidize in excess of 41 billion taxpayer dollars to aid/help other countries...
- *However,* we *can* spent 683 billion dollars on defense 2017 alone.

- *However*, we *can* spend more than 6 trillion dollars in 10 years in Afghanistan and Iraq!
- *However,* we *can* afford to spend between *100-300 billion* taxpayer dollars each and every year on those who have crashed our borders! To this, I say,

How can we NOT invest in our own children!???

- *To do nothing*, is to sign off on the future detriment and well being on all of our babies...
- *To do nothing,* is to further cultivate those murky cesspools in our future, breeding more potential psychopaths. Let us drain that swamp, expose, then clean up the muck and save our children...
- *To do nothing* brings to mind one of the simplest and most profound quotations from the bible,... *"and Jesus wept..." John, 11:35.*

It is absolutely vital that we severe the insidious head of "child abuse" in our country...

To this, I rest my case...

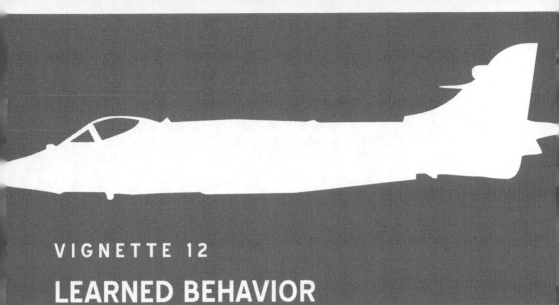

VIGNETTE 12

LEARNED BEHAVIOR

The power of negative expectations

Once upon a time, there was a relatively successful quarterback. This guy was an above average athlete in many ways. He had a great collegiate career and shared his alma mater with his franchise owner. He had a long nine year career of "almost winning the big game!".

It was 4th and goal, his team was down by two points with only seconds left in the game. This was the big one, for all the marbles and a berth to the playoffs. He had worked the clock like a pro, setting his team up for an easy 3 point chip shot to win the game.

This quarterback also happened to be the ball holder for the veteran field goal kicker. With a few seconds left, the seasoned longball snapper shoots a perfect strike right into his hands. The ball is fumbled and the clock runs out as the "ball holding" quarterback picks up his fumble. Only to be plummeted as he tries to run around end. Game over! His team loses yet another opportunity.

Throughout his entire career, he racks up impressive offensive numbers, only to lose the game by throwing into a pick six at the end of the game. But they were so close! If only this guy hadn't thrown 2-3 interceptions!

I recall several years into this Q.B.'s career, seeing the defensive coordinators, always in a fit of rage, running up and down the sidelines. His defense had done their job as usual and once again, his quarterback throws yet another pick six. Another opportunity was lost to advance into the playoffs.

This particular quarterback, throughout his career, exhibited classic symptoms of a disorder known in psychiatric terms as "learned behavior". This is a characteristic exhibited by adult-children throughout their lives. Unless curtailed by therapeutic counselling, it is a self-fulfilling, self-perpetuating cycle of self-destruction.

It is an extension from our early stymied development of our superegos. In failing to achieve approval or acceptance from our parents, we turn our frustration onto ourselves and become our own worst critic. Simply put, our inner child is never able to mature in a healthy manner. This coupled with the toxicity of continuous passive-aggressive abandonment, verbal and violent abuse, we grow into adult-children with a devastated self-esteem.

"Learned behavior" is our consciousness, subconsciously reconnecting with our negative reinforcements suppressed limbic memories.

In this portion of our psyche's are stored all of the negative tapes from our traumatic stress events. As a means of self-preservation, we suppress these traumas and lock them away… As we fumble through adult-childhood, we subconsciously make decisions that destroy our potential. We continually sabotage any successes in our lives. In a twisted and nauseating manner this tendency gives trouble souls a sense of completeness…

This quarterback I used to illustrate this behavior pattern is strictly conjecture. It just so happens that his behavior patterns align perfectly with all the traits of this "learned behavioral" disorder. Almost always at the brink of success, he snatches defeat from the jaws of victory.

Perhaps you know someone that exhibits these self-destructive tendencies? Excelling in many ways, only to do something to wipe out our potential. Someone who appears to be incapable of enjoying life in a state of happiness and self contentment. Always listening to those negative inner critics, they act out to destroy all that is good and well in their lives. In a twisted sort of way, this fulfills the *negative expectations* coming from an abusive and toxic childhood.

Imagine if you can, a childhood filled with venomous vile…

"Your as useless as teats on a wart hog! You'll never amount to anything! Your a worthless piece of excrement! When you grow up, your going to be a worthless ditch digger! Your a stupid idiot, an imbecile!...". "but mom, I'm thirsty..." "How bout I come back there and spit in your mouth!"...

After self-destructing, we feel useless, worthless and lowly insignificant. Yet we somehow sense the warm glow of well being, as if we are one with our universe. "How can I have a sense of contentment after fucking up my life, yet one more time!?". Our dysfunctional underdeveloped superego is a petulant pouting inner child... our own worst critic...

Its oxymoronic!!!

How can there be *ANY* contentment in destroying your potential??? Therein lays the classic paradox that a majority of the "walking wounded" and that PTSD child abuse survivors have to cope with. We, forever continue to bash our heads against the "glass ceiling" of "learned behavior"...

When ever I disclose to anyone that I have PTSD, the standard response is, "were you in the military?"... This is a common misconception!... One does not have to have been a "wounded warrior" to suffer from PTSD!

Child abuse can be just as devastating to our psyches as the horrors of war...

We are subconsciously satisfying our negative inner voices buried deep in our limbic brain system. We fumble throughout our lives never realizing how our brains are wired and are functioning. Consequently, we go through our lives squandering hope and opportunities... "Learned behavior" is a common denominator and nemesis for all abused kids who grow into adult children.

Those negative tapes are as real as the air we breath.

They will continue to have control of our conscious thought processes...

Unless we... *DO SOMETHING ABOUT IT!!!*

Go to a local used book store and buy a couple of used paperback books for $9. Attempt to self-heal with "Cognitive processing therapy" or " "Cognitive behavioral therapy". If you can arrange it, see a psychotherapist to help in guiding your healing process.

Please, don't go through another day of self-abuse. Hope springs eternal for those that attempt to help themselves. Self-affirmation is the first step to recovery therapy for "the walking wounded"... In our Father's eyes, we all have value...

Won't you PLEASE come walk with me?...

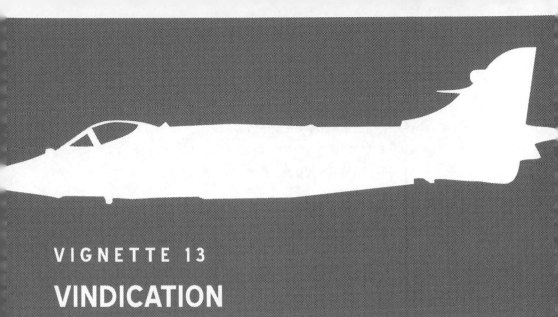

VIGNETTE 13
VINDICATION

Adult-children grow up, desperately craving love and attention, constantly excelling at many endeavors or activities. All in an effort to seek approval from parents incapable of giving it, we constantly strive to achieve perfection in everything we do. All in a futile attempt to gain even a modicum of positive reinforcement. In failing to fill our emotional voids, inevitably, we resort to self destruction. We become our own worst critic. We continue throughout our lives, sabotaging our successes.

Perhaps you know someone like this. Perhaps you see it in yourself... This could be an "Ah Ha moment for you?!". I had a similar, destiny moment researching the after effects of complex PTSD. Just recently, in this crystalizing moment, I realized that I had been suffering from extreme PTSD for almost my entire life.

I was an abused child...

succumbing to "learned behavioral" disorder my entire life...

Who I am and my life's experiences are of *NO* consequence! Exposing a brutally detailed account of my narrative is my attempt at self therapy.

Also, to illustrate how undiagnosed PTSD can mastitize itself onto our psyches as well as wreak havoc on our health.

I refuse to let it define my existence and in no way am I intending to play "the victim card". Additionally, I will refuse any invitation to any "pity parties"!...

This is in no way, shape or form, an attempt to cast blame or judgement on anyone, nor is it a massive rationalization, period, end of paragraph!...

This is very simply a concerted effort and attempt to match insidious, illogical behavior with abusive toxic circumstances and explain...

- *How* a lifetime of undiagnosed symptoms of PTSD can detrimentally affect our health and invariably lead to death.
- *How* a childhood, consumed by physical and emotional maltreatment and mental turmoil can have just as severe of consequences as the horrors of war...
- *How* the human mind can rally and heal itself, developing coping skills so that we may press on in this human enterprise we call life...
- *How* self enlightenment can open "Pandora's box" to a deeply scarred psyche. *Pandora is a reference to Greek mythology, wherein it's opening generates many more complicated problems as the result of unwise interferences.*
- To help illustrate how courageously facing down your deepest, darkest most appalling secrcts is absolutely paramount to our psychological healing.

It is with these thoughts at the forefront of my intentions, I delve into the inner regions of a deeply scarred and tormented psyche... my own.

I moved from an undisclosed Air Force base in an undisclosed military strategic command. Therein I attended a private College Prep Catholic high school in my hometown, Space City U.S.A.. St. Bernard's Catholic Academy for boys. I lived with my grandparents on the fighter pilot's wife's side of my family. My grandmother was the mother image I had lacked my entire childhood.

She loved and doted over me. She always showed affection with hugs and kisses. Grandma glowed with the Grace of God throughout her life. I felt blessed to be in such a loving place. I worked 24-32 hours a week at a local supermarket to pay for tuition, books and board for my food. I recall each semester running around $800 plus books. I recall making an hourly wage of $4.25, thinking I was in high cotton.

Sometime during the beginning of my senior year, my parents received a call at their undisclosed military strategic command. This is was my family's final military station. It was from an academic advisor for the advancement of mexican american studies. The fighter pilot's wife answered. Mr. Lopez introduced himself and let her know that he was calling to let them know that your son had distinguished himself scholastically and was eligible for a collegiate academic scholarship. He went on to say that "you should be very proud of your son".

The fighter pilot's wife, in a nonchalant manner said, "yeah, yeah, yeah" as if to appear to be brushing off a salesman with an ulterior motive. Very quickly the advisor replied, *"This is a really BIG DEAL!"*, then asked to speak with my father.

Colonel fighter pilot took the line. The advisor explained the significance and weight of this distinction. "Your son, in the first semester to his senior year is ranked 26th in a class of 125 in one of the most prestigious private college prep Catholic high schools in the nation.

To add to his accomplishment, his curriculum was steeped heavily in STEM, science, technology, engineering and mathematics. The advanced sciences of physics, chemistry, biology, oceanography and geology. This, along with Algebra, trig & geometry, elementary analysis and pre-calculus to boot. Adding merit to my accomplishment is that I was considered to be in a minority class.

Growing up on air force bases all over the world, I never realized I was a minority until, I moved back to my hometown.

I remember my grandfather on the phone with Dad..." I don't understand it, I never see him crack a book!" I always did my homework on campus, before I drove to work in the afternoon. Usually arriving home late at night to the loving comfort of my grandparents.

Grandma, smiling in her rocker, Pearl beer in hand in her dark room. The only light emanating from her black and white TV, viewing local wrestling. Grandpa in this dark room, hooked up to his respirator, watching the same program. It was there that I felt loved and safe. I was basking in the paternal glow from my grandparents love.

Somehow I knew that I was vindicated, I was not a stupid idiot after all… Holding true to "learned behavior", I procrastinated and missed the deadline for applying for this scholastic opportunity.

Much later in my corporate struggles in futility, I was injured, preventing asset losses while managing a "big box" supermarket. The victims of crime association gave me a timed cognitive I.Q. exam. I finished at the ring of the bell.

Later on when I met with my counsellor, I was informed, "I have been giving these tests for 30 years. I have never had anyone complete this test and let alone ACE it!". He went on to let me know that he had never seen such a strong and driven work ethic and that I was in the top 15% intelligence quotient in the country. Ill defined superegos tend to be obsessed with overachieving as consummate workaholics. Hyperproductivity and an obsessive attention to detail is the direct symptom from a deficient superego. To coin a phrase, we tend to be "anal attentive"…

The state was prepared to pay for all the tuition and supplemental expenses of my re-education's choosing. "If you wish to go back to school to become a brain surgeon", the state is ready to pay. This was yet another validation of sorts, however I had a young son and wife to provide for. Fumbling through the fog of "learned behavior", I pressed on. Once more, I could discern a vague sense of vindication.

Flashing backwards, I enrolled at the alma mater of my father, one semester late, only to descend to scholastic probation in record time. Instead of attending college I should have enrolled into intensive full time psychotherapy.

Truth be told, I was suffering from extreme and chronic symptoms of PTSD with the subsequent anxiety and depression thereof. Laying in my dorm bunk for a week at a time, scared to death of facing the world, let alone the *social* challenges of campus academia. I was suffering from an antisocial personality disorder cultivated from a toxic childhood of extreme abuse and emotional neglect. I was thrust into an unfamiliar environment with an extreme phobia of people. Even though I was intellectually and academically qualified, I was psychologically and emotionally ill equipped…

After leaving University, I returned to Space City U.S.A. to work in the only business I had experience in the supermarket industry. At 19, I bought a two story, five bedroom, 3 bathroom home in distress conditions.

One had only to look beyond the dead cat to realize it's potential. So what that it needed a new roof, a new A/C unit, new fencing, three thousand square feet of new carpet, new paint inside and out, major sheetrock repair, outside siding, new kitchen and reconstructed garage. Holding true to *"learned behavior"*, I then paid top market dollar for it. What a deal!

I was to become an expert at buying high and selling low. Two of my college buddies moved in with me. Before long, I had somewhat of an animal house going on.

Throughout my corporate careers, I continually excelled, marked as an extreme overachiever. At one point, I was even described as a "superstar.", only to self-destruct with an unauthorised absence now and again.

This was my subconscious, sabotaging my successes through my *"learned behavior disorder"*.

Those were the unrelenting inner voices stored away in the hippocampus of my brain. *"your a stupid idiot! You'll never amount to anything! When you grow up your going to be a worthless ditch digger!"*

After 12 years of banging my head against the invisible barrier of *"learned behavior"*, I got my bachelor's degree from "The University of Hard Knocks". I branched out into middle management as a District Sales Manager with petroleum retail corporations.

I majored in "kicking ass and taking names". I got positive results through training and empowering my people. This, in an industry where senior management was known to kill and devour their young, every two years,… all in the name of salary justification.

My head strong petulant inner child stumbled his way through a number of corporate endeavors. To the untrained eye, it would appear that I was being canned more than tuna… I was merely fulfilling my "learned behavioral" tendencies. After a 12 year stent in "big box" retail management, I averaged 3-5 year tenures in a few corporate ventures, eventually going into business for myself.

At that point, I barely got my son through six years of college at my father's alma mater. I had two to three businesses during this period of my life. As Bernie Jr. got closer to graduation, one by one, my businesses failed.

With a real estate license in hand, I had purchased a four bedroom home in Bernie Jr.s University town. We rented out rooms to help pay for my son's room and board. At this time, I had two more mortgages in my hometown. I had become a realtor and a property manager of sorts.

At one point, I actually recall hearing those inner critical voices whispering, *"this is unstainable, you'll never amount to anything!", "you're a stupid idiot!,... remember?!"*.

Truth be told, I sacrificed everything, bankrupting my good credit standings to push my son up to graduation day. One by one I either sold at a loss or broke- even on all my properties. The market was extremely soft and I had to get my cost of living down to its *lowest* common denominator. I bought an RV and morphed into the "old man that lived in a shoe". With diminishing cash flow, all my financial priorities were diverted to getting my son through just a couple more years of college.

"Learned behavior" had made certain that I would never become a real estate multi-thousandaire. This mattered not! I had achieved the goal of realizing my son through college,... at what should have been my alma mater.

This was without a doubt the proudest moment of my life. I basked vicariously in the glow of my son's success. All those 12-14 hour days, 7 days a week for more than six years had finally paid off in spades.

So if you find yourself feeling anxious, depressed, angry and easily irritated, seek help with counseling. These are primary symptoms from PTSD. If you have you ever found yourself resenting someones prolonged stare, thinking to yourself, *"what the hell are you looking at?!, "*, this is merely your *"learned behavior"* parroting your abuser...

If you find yourself sabotaging your successes or feeling extremely insecure or even severely depressed, seek help from a therapist. You can break the cycle. It's never too late.

At 12 years of age, I swore to myself that if I ever have children, I would never raise a hand to them... I was destined and determined to break the insidious cycle of transgeneral child abuse!...

At 62, my psychotherapist gave me a 20 questionnaire, exposing what I had recently discovered to be true. My symptoms for PTSD scored off the charts. I had been unknowingly and silently suffering from extreme *posttraumatic stress disorder* my entire life.

VIGNETTE 14

WORDS MATTER!

In emotionally damaged children, the outer edges of the cortex, the limbic portion of the brain, the hippocampus stores all of our negative tapes. They're etched deeply into our psychological DNA.

As a child, we are implicitly incapable of rationalizing our traumatic stress. So in order to cope, we simply bury them in the limbic portions of our brains... *Subconsciously,* trauma takes control of our conscious thoughts and actions. These negatives tapes stay with us for a lifetime.

I had endured nearly an entire childhood, eight to nine years of negative verbal bashings such as, "God damn you!...You stupid idiot!". This coupled with regular brutal beatings, eventually the semantics began to evolve.

In her growing frustration and furry the fighter pilot's wife had introduced an unfamiliar word,... "imbecile!". At eleven, I had to go to a dictionary for this one. Webster defined it as a "stupid idiot". Why did this not surprise me?... Isn't that redundant?

"When you grow up, you'll never amount to anything!,,,WHAM!... You stupid idiot! BAM!... You imbecile! POW!... You had better wipe that smirk off your face! WHAM!... I'm going to beat the tar out of you! BAM!... When you grow up, your going to be a worthless ditch digger! POW!

A ditch digger?!?!"...

What? *How can she possibly know that?!*

Truth be known, the fighter pilot's wife realized I was growing into a man. After eight to nine years of brutal battering, she realized I was getting too big to be emasculated. I had refused to relinquish my alpha identity. I had refused to have my will broken. Such insolence grated and gnawed at her incessantly...

For whatever vindictive and malicious intentions, she felt compelled to resort to negative projections into my future. "You'll never amount to anything! When you grow up, you're going to be a worthless ditch digger!...". All those years of emotional lambasting and routine physical torture sessions were futile to her objective.

She had failed.

This, in and of itself, added to the fighter pilot's wife's furry and unrelenting determination... She could not break me, as I never had shed a tear, aside from the initial *traumatic bath tub assault and battery at four years of age...*

Every time she came at me arm raised with such contempt, I felt like I was about to encounter an old enemy... She would scream vile, verbal abuses, intermittently followed up by a barrage of relentless "heavy metal coat hanger" lashings...

I remember thinking, "Do all first born sons go through this? Is this the norm?"... *"Is a mother's love supposed to hate, hurt and torment?!".*

Well it must have been the case, as I never heard a word from my father. During my entire childhood of physical, psychological and emotional abuse, I never, ever heard a single, solitary word from my father!!!...

The fighter pilot's wife had complete and total carte blanche in my child mismanagement . To even think of exposing this matter was unspeakable!!!... The thought of doing so just might invoke a double jeopardy. l chose to remain silent, as 90% of all abused children do. I chose my defensive lines very carefully... Defending one front would be much easier than fighting on two fronts...

My young, tender heart, gently and silently wept...

I was in a prolonged, *private* battle for my self preservation. I was in a "one on one" series of sustained standoffs. All for the right to exist and resist the perils of a monstrous tyrannical authority... my mother.

I was destined to grow into an adult-child with an extreme disdain for authority; fear of rejection; distrust of women and with a devastated self-esteem.

At the age of 12 years, at the conclusion of this one particular beatdown, *in a gesture of finality,* the fighter pilot's wife uttered these words,

"I wish you had never been born!!!"

I thought that I had inoculated myself from any further pain that she might have inflicted. I thought I had masked myself from the emotional daggers of all those years of utter abuse... " You stupid idiot! Imbecile! Worthless ditch digger!". Then she uttered those words,

... wishing me out of existence...

It was as if a two by four had physically struck me in the gut! I felt my diaphragm physically retract, forcing all the air from my lungs. It took me several moments to digest these words and more than a lifetime to assess the psychological damage done. To that date in time, at 12 years of age I had never felt so alone and isolated...

WORDS MATTER!

Physical wounds will heal. The good Lord made us in His own image, resilient and self-healing. Vile words, especially during our entire childhood, cut like a razor to the marrow of our psyche. Words raised against our fledgling minds exact a lifetime's worth of mental turmoil... The extreme essense of helplessness, coupled with the intense and utter darkness of hopelessness, seemed insurmountable... To this end, these words fail to encapsulate...

These are wounds that will never completely heal, leaving jagged scars that last more than a lifetime. Self help and therapy can help to rationalize and minimize dark trauma.

Although almost a year of weekly therapy has helped in exposing and resurrecting traumatic memories, those dark shadowed voices never truly go away. The hurt never completely subsides. In time and through many months of therapy, our pain merely diminishes by varying degrees.

The fighter pilot's wife simply walked away from me this day, never to physically or verbally abuse me again...

Her methods turned to more subtle, subversive and psychological tactics. It was as if her sole purpose in my life was to demean and diminish my existence.

As an abused child, having developed a rather high degree of survival intuition, I could sense her resentment for my mere existence. It was as if I were a continuing irritation and reminder of my insolence, like a thorn in her side... It was as if my "state of being" was a constant annoyance to her, as I was the only witness to her incessant "darkside"... To the fighter pilot's wife, my mere presence was a rude and disrespectful threat to her absolute authority.

In her realm, her power was absolute... The fighter pilot was a mere puppet and she was the puppet master. She was the primary enforcer. On rare occasions, she would delegate corporal punishments to him. "Just you wait till your father comes home!!!". She gave the command to "sick him!" and he would attack... There was never anyone adult enough to say, "why don't we examine all the facts and assess a resolution to this conflict?". The fighter pilot's wife had complete absolute power and authority. We existed in a medieval hierarchy where the Queen was judge, jury and executioner. Retribution for perceived insolence was shift and emmediate.

Be that as it may, from that day forward, I was barely acknowledged with a minimal amount of tolerance. I was to become an inconvenient nuisance... Suddenly "wishing me out of existence" had a new and rather profound relevance. At 12 years of age, my survival instincts had given me wisdom well beyond my years.

I had become a non-entity, reduced to a fraction of a person... She had completely washed her hands of me... as I was the only witness to her persistently hateful and monstrous darkside. There was no escaping it...

There was no way out!!!

From this day forward, I was taken off of the fighter pilot's wife's radar... with a minimal amount of acknowledgement...

In public, we were the epitome of the perfect family, and all, oh so well behaved. Each, one of eight, scared to death of the consequences for any social missteps.

At the end of that day, I sorely welcomed the absence of her attention... From this distant vantage point, I saw a physically exhausted and emotionally emaciated, extremely angry youngman. All that remained was the empty shell of a deeply disturbed non entity with a calloused and hardened heart.

Truth be told, after 8-9 brutal, emotionally draining years, my will was dangling by a thread... Although I felt that she had failed to break me, there was most definitely, no cause for celebration. Her work had been done.

On the surface, I may have appeared to be *unbroken*... In reality, she had shattered my self esteem and simply walked away. Truth be told, I was emotionally disemboweled, eviscerated at 4 years of age, splish splashing in a bathtub.

At 12 years of age, I felt like I had endured a lifelong marathon of emotional, psychological and physical abuse.

In recollection and in seeking the truth through therapy, I shared with my therapist one of several personal moments with the fighter pilot's wife.

I was around 5 ½ years of age during the Christmas season. We were going somewhere in our family car, as "Rudolph the red nosed reindeer" had just played on the radio. I asked, " Mom, where is history?"

She completely ignored me...

I noticed my therapist's facial expression cringe...

It was as if I wasn't even there... My refusal to acquiesce to my mothers abusive attempts at emasculation was on full display. It was as if I were totally invisible.

Because I stood up to her incessant abuse, in her mind's eye, I wasn't worth giving the time of day... I shrugged it off and was content that I would never, ever in my entire childhood have a single, solitary conversation with the fighter pilot's wife.

When ever in her presence, my cortisol hormone levels were in a heightened state. In that light, I gingerly walked on eggshells, trying *NEVER* to make eye contact!... Doing so could invariably provoke a reminder of my insolence and yet another series of undeserved assault and battery... Hypervigilance was the summation of my entire childhood and early adolescence...

I was simply content *not* to be the object of her monstrous ire. Always mindful, whenever within arms length of her. Whenever in her shadow, I always made full use of my peripheral vision. My spidey senses were always full on... Hypersensitivity and vigilance had become crucial to my self-preservation.

Simply put, I was shell-shocked as if I had been in a protracted and bloody war... PTSD was my norm and my modus operandi was existing with cortisol stress hormone rushes... Stress was a constant companion for me... The absence of pain and mental torment was my solace. In those intermittent moments of tranquility I could sigh and breathe deeply... Bliss was very simply, the absence of her anger... My young heart desperately pined for the love and affection of a mother figure... My entire life would be void of this sensation...

The fighter pilot's wife had an unforgiving disposition. She had been known to hold grudges for a lifetime. Albeit, She was also capable of extremely amiable moments with incredible amounts of generosity and compassion.

Just not towards her first born son...

Whenever she made negative mental notations on someone, they were always done irrevocably in ink. In her mind's eye, I was permanently blotted out of her life...

My psychiatrist, asked that with 7 siblings, how my abuse was ever not noted. I explained that most of my siblings were unborn or too young to know any better.

Hell... I didn't realize myself that my own brutal mistreatment was unacceptable! At 4 ½ and throughout my childhood, the entire realm of my world was stamped, sealed and confined to the four walls of our home. *I was compelled to desperately cling to that which was electrocuting me!...*

In varying degrees, we were probably all victims of the "helsinki syndrome". With lightning in our bones, we had pledged total allegiance to she who held us captive...

Other than that, her moments of conflict were carefully chosen. As I grew older, she always approached me when I was isolated from the pride. Divide, separate then pounce was her strategy. To this day, as siblings, we tend to remain socially isolated from one another. A definite symptom from being held captive to a "Helsinki syndrome" and a prolonged exposure to a sociopathic, antisocial environment... The ill defined superego's of our inner children kept us socially isolated. This was a directly proportional consequence to our emotional famine... We were all starving for even a modicum of love and attention!...

I recall in my multitude of prepubescent beatings, wishing I that was larger in physical stature. Bigger, so that I might rise up and *SMASH* my abuser!!! This was followed by immediate and extreme sensations of guilt... My therapist comforted me saying, "that reprisal was a natural reaction for children in extreme peril"...

I had been moulded into a scrappy and stubborn little fighter, with a tenacious will to survive and resist authority... As molten metal is seared and beaten into steel, my young heart was tempered and hardened with a great deal of incredulity... Disbelief and doubt had displaced all my capacity for *LOVE and TRUST*...

Of the three possible responses to terror,... pause, fight or flight, I always chose to bow up, stand my ground and fight. Adrenaline and cortisol hormone rushes were a constant throughout my life. I fought back by taking a defensive posture, throwing up my right forearm as a defensive shield, blocking each and every blow from whatever her weapon of choice was on that day. More times than not, it was a stiff, metal coat hanger. To this day, I own *NOT ONE* metal hanger!

My psychiatrist explains this duality and contradiction in mother's personality, very simply as... *We are all complicated individuals.*

How could such a *simple minded* explanation justify a lifetime of torment and unrelenting self examination.

Unless someone had walked a mile in my shoes, how the *HELL* could anyone make such an insensitive and obtuse statement? How can a priest give marital advice having never been married? Unless he has woken up each and every morning next to the love of his life, how is that possible?... Life's experiences trump the theoretical anytime anywhere. Being at the receiving end of a "full metal lashing" is an experience that can not be learned from a textbook... Where does empathy fit into this equation?... Dump the couches!!!... Sense and sensitivity should be a prerequisite to psychiatry...

Trying to rationalize the contradictions of emotional duality leads to a lifetime of mental turmoil and quandary.

- Why do I always feel wholly inadequate?
- Why do I always feel helplessly and hopelessly flawed?
- Why is it that anger lingers immediately below my personas surface?
- Why is it so natural for my mind to constantly drift and dwell on the negative aspects of my life... and then campout! They are resurrected in never ending, recurring nightmares.
- Why do I feel so broken on the inside, like damaged goods?
- Why do I gravitate toward self-hate and self revulsion?

Like reruns from a bad movie, those negative tapes play over and over again, to the point of hopelessness, anger, anxiety and frustrated depression... Trying to process and frame these "obvious contradictions" with any logic or reasoning is like trying to work a mental "Rubik's Cube"! The only solution to my puzzlement was well outside the realm of my mental understanding. It is an absolute lesson in futility.

The only reality I knew was that I was routinely getting the *hell beat out of me* my entire childhood. Somehow I managed to survive and grow a heart with a tremendous amount of compassion and capacity for love, helping and healing. The only hell in my entire precarious predicament was being projected from within my abuser... My "Mother dearest!"...

In my reality, she would change her moods on a dime and come at me, always with the same fire and fury in her rhetoric and physical stamina. It was as if she would flip a switch into "attack mode"... With the final lashing and verbal bashing, she would flip off that same switch, compose herself, take a deep breathe, straighten her hair then go back to her cigarettes, coffee and soaps... It was as if nothing had ever happened...

She possessed the ability to completely disconnect from one persona and switch to another. All the while, completely suspending logic and reason from her hateful and hurtful actions… It was then that she would continue ignoring me for another 3-4 months. Like clockwork, this sociopathic exercise in futility bordering insanity would repeat itself throughout my entire childhood and early adolescence…

These thought processes are the aftershocks and imbedded observations from a war torn childhood. They are symptomatic from sociopathic fallout born from relentless negative reinforcement throughout a toxic and abusive childhood.

They are therapeutically labeled as *"stuck points"*, probably because they stick in one's head for a lifetime. They forever dwell in the hippocampus of our limbic system, our brains. The only relief from their pain is to therapeutically acknowledge their existence and re-affirming oneself on how they got there.

*Cognitive, rational thinking…*knowledge and understanding is the key to the doorway of explaining the unexplainable.

Even then, after 12 months of weekly cognitive behavioral therapy, the pain lessens and diminishes, but only by degrees.

The trick is to, very simply not mind that it hurts…

Through almost an entire childhood of physical abuse, I was able to completely disconnect myself from physical pain. Verbal, emotional and psychological pain is far more difficult to process and compartmentalize…

This, in and of itself, opens up an entirely different set of questions.

- Why do I have such an overwhelming disdain for authority?
- Why do I have so much difficulty with the trust of women?
- Why is it that a mother's love can feel both painful and contemptuous?
- Why am I so reluctant to open up and expose my feelings?
- Why am I scared to death of rejection?

- Why do I continually avoid relationships and readily hit my ejection button? (a preemptive defensive mechanism to avoid rejection)
- Why do I throw up a forearm when someone unexpectedly screams?

These are all symptomatic questions brought on by a lifetime of posttraumatic stress. Soothing the unresolved suffering is a lifelong work in progress...

VIGNETTE 15

GO TO A HAPPY PLACE!...
THEN FORGIVE!

If you think that sharing my childhood to be easy, you couldn't be further from the truth! Sharing these abhorrent microcosms into my childhood is more excruciating than words can describe.

As I had mentioned earlier, I am mortally ashamed and embarrassed by my past. I have been reprocessing bouts of recurring anxiety attacks as I probe into my slumbering memories. Feeling the increased palpitation of my heart and labored breathing are mere symptoms from the stress of anxiety.

Hurtful, haunting voices are deeply ingrained and remain in the memories banks of PTSD, induced by toxic child abuse...

Depression, born from PTSD has a snowballing effect. If one allows it to take hold, it will linger on and on into a perpetual state of darkness. One day of listlessness in bed can turn into three and then a week or more... if we let it. It can rob us of the simple pleasures in our lives and in extreme cases, snatch the life right out of us...

"Today my forest is dark. The trees are sad and the butterflies fragile wings have all been broken...". "All it takes is a beautiful, fake smile to hide

an injured soul and they will never notice how broken you really are!"...
Robin Williams.

As a weekly assignment, my therapist had asked me to do something
for enjoyment. To self indulge myself in a "taster's choice moment" for
just myself. After a week of trying to think of something I enjoyed doing,
I kept drawing blanks. I had always drawn comfort from simply being a
workaholic.

In our next therapy session, I said that, "I had thought about taking
in a bullfight on acid,, but decided, nah... that would be too much of a
stretch.". At which point, I admitted, in a quandary that there must be
something wrong with the reward sensory receptors in my brain. More
than likely a lack of dopamine. My therapist laughed, explaining that this
was a common denominator among those that suffer from depression born
of PTSD. We tend to be unable to experience euphoric sensations.

Thinking back throughout my life, I always had a hard time thinking
of any activities that would actually " blow my skirt up". All that readily
came to mind were the negative stuck points, all those hurtful, self
deprecating, degrading thoughts...

Forcing these traumatic memories to the surface is painfully paramount
to the grieving and healing process. This, in and of itself is what makes
therapy so excruciatingly difficult. As if I were digging and probing into
a gaping throbbing wound...

*The sharing of my life's narrative is a deeply chagrined attempt
to lend a voice to the abused adult-children of this world...*

There are potentially 70-80 million of us, each and every generation!
The next time you gaze into a crowd of people, know that 1 in 5 have
suffered and survived a traumatic childhood... 20% or more! We are, all of
us, wounded and embarrassed to the point of silence. We are all members
of the "walking wounded", a silent yet pervasive and growing minority...

*Standing witness to the horrors of war is a minuscule percentage of our
population. There is no comparison to the pervasive and overwhelming number
of those suffering in the silent desperation of an abusive and toxic childhood...*

All the symptoms from extreme PTSD, born from child abuse are a
normal consequence to an *abnormal* cause and effect.

There is never anything normal or more grotesquely
abhorrent than the torturing of a child!

"Fathers, do not provoke your children, lest they become discouraged." Colossians 3:21

Placing these thoughts and experiences into writing is to open myself up to a flurry of stinging rebukes! Like a swarm of angry hornets, they attack my conscious thought processes from every direction.

Throughout my entire childhood, I felt as if I was drowning in a crowded pool… and no one would throw me a lifeline. Now I find myself, near the end of my days trying my best to accurately *describe the water* to benefit those that may have tread in those same treacherous waters....

PTSD forever fosters anger, just beneath the surface. One's mental thought processes always tend to navigate to negative thoughts and stuck points, and then camp out... All those negative tapes manifest themselves in our subconscious. They continually come to us in our dreams, playing over and over, like a broken record. They constantly replay moments of regret and oftentimes excruciating experiences. These nightmares are triggers to PTSD and make for rather rude frightening and angry awakenings… We wake up frustrated and angry at ourselves for not being able to change the outcome in our dream state. The responses run the full gamut our emotional range, sad, glad, mad, scared, ashamed and disgusted.

Harnessing my emotions to illuminate a tabooed subject much larger than the sum total of myself is my design intent… that being "toxic child abuse"...

This is most certainly one of the most difficult and most excruciating endeavors of my life. The bearing of my soul and sharing of my most appalling secrets is mortifying, yet necessary. Necessary to my mental well being and healing...

Before I leave this earth, it is my utmost desire to share with you, a disturbingly detailed and brutally honest vision into my psyche. To share an intimate, unvarnished account of my traumas, is to help you understand that you are not alone!

I am certain that many of you have much more ghastly experiences that will never be told. *Quantifying our torture is most definitely not my intent.*

My childhood, by all intents and purposes is *NOTHING* compared to literally tens of millions of the walking wounded, the adult-children in this world. My life's trauma is dwarfed by theirs'.

I have been chauffeuring "rideshares" long enough to have had several fares confide in me, sharing their horror stories, much worse than mine.

I keep a copy of "Cognitive behavioral therapy for dummies"on my dashboard. This, in and of itself has opened up many individual conversations locked away in Pandora's box.

Those that have survived as adult children, when gentilly nudged, hunger to share their pent up anguish and pain. They readily open up and out spews a geyser of childhood atrocities.

Kids that had been thrown through sheetrock walls, kids being used to extinguish cigars and cigs, as ashtrays! Kids being knocked unconscious with a can of projectiled green beans for mumbling back to their mother, only to be consoled upon reawakening, "see what happens when you talk back to your mother!". "You're a stupid idiot!", "You're an imbecile!", "When you grow up, you're going to be a worthless ditch digger!". We won't even attempt to expose the sexual horrors. The *unspeakable* list of brutal acts have no end or moral boundary…

This just in, June 2019!… Somewhere in this "coast to coast" country of ours, a sperm donor punches his five year old son in the head, killing him instantly.

Why?!...

What is it about the tormented dysfunctional mind set that would compel a father to commit such a heinous act?… The boy had eaten *HIS* piece of "fathers day" cake… "Learned behavior"…

Just last month, in east Texas, 2 year old Tommy Sullivan is beaten into a vegitative state by his mother's boyfriend. The abusing douchebag received two consecutive life sentences while Tommy's mother got 10 years probation. Poor little Tommy got a lifetime sentence of free HBO, medical, room and board as a ward of the state of Texas.

This, just one more nauseating statistic of the 2500 children that we murder and each and every year!!!... One more sickening annual statistic of the nearly 7.4 million reported cases of kids that are physically injured in this country of ours... Someone should write a book on this stuff!... Ohhh!...

Up from the bowels of hell, these nauseating and atrocious acts crash through transgenerational barriers and infect the next generation... It's vile, putrid stench permeates our nostrils and violates every sense of our moral consciousness. These toxic bashings and abuses are endless and in every case are an extension from the previous generation...

These are NOT human traits that are intentionally taught, although it may appear that many abusive adults recite verbatim from the same manual..."Child abuse for dummies and @#!!?#&"!'s". All of these violent traits and tendencies are merely recurring reflections from a violent and twisted childhood...

Just the other night I had picked up a young couple in their 20"s. During the course of their fare I asked him what he did for *a* living. *He replied that he was very simply a cook in a trailer. In an attempt to bolster his esteem I suggested that "no, you are a chef". He replied that, "No just a cook. It beats the hell out of being a ditch digger!...". I thought "what an odd thing to say"* as it had struck a painful and highly personal chord with me. I had to ask him, " Why would you say such a thing?". To which he replied, " During my entire childhood and adolescence, my parents always told me that I was worthless. That I would never amount to anything more than a worthless "ditch digger"!"...

It was then and there that I realized that the "Unholy grail", "Child abuse for Dummies and @#!!?#&"!'s", actually does exist!... These very same words had been exacted against me during my entire childhood...

Through "learned behavior", these traits are instilled into the psychological DNA of the afflicted. These abusive tendencies mirror a grotesque sense of satisfaction from a twisted and sickening quest for misplaced revenge.

This, in and of itself perpetuates the cycle from our tormentors... Hence, the cycle of twisted vengeance tends to repeat itself... Infecting future generations to come. 50% of these abused children grow up to correlate with an abusive partner, who themselves were abused. "Learned behavior"... It's a self perpetuating generational cycle to a lifetime of human misery and degradation. It is as unnatural a progression as "mother nature" could contrive. These shared violations are merely a minuscule number of vile acts in this vast underworld of child torture.

Why not call it what it is?!

We are all walking zombies, fumbling our way through a foggy maze… constantly bouncing off of the dead end walls of "learned behavior", *silently screaming out in guttural anguish.*

"WHY ME!?!"…

There are multitudes that have endured *much, MUCH, MUCH* worse abuse from both parents! *May God help them all!* It is my sincere wish that you realize… that in every case of dysfunction,

YOU ARE NOT ALONE! IT IS NOT YOUR FAULT!

Please seek professional guidance. Invest in a few paperbacks to attempt to self heal. Self-acknowledgement is the first step in self realization. Learn forgiveness,

"forgive us our trespasses as we forgive those who trespasses against us".

If you don't believe in God, that's okay, because he believes in you!…

Read up on "Cognitive processing therapy" and complex PTSD then work through the daily exercises.

GO TO A HAPPY PLACE! You are a winner! You are a good person! It's not your fault! You are a success! You are NOT a loser! You are smart! You are not an imbecile! When you hear those haunting negative inner voices, counter them with a chorus of positive affirmations, a barrage of positive reinforcement.

You were made in our Makers divine image! You are a creation of our supreme Father! You deserve that promotion! Your a GREAT person! People respect and look up to you! You deserve all the accolades intended by God our Father!

As those reviled voices start to tear you down, counter them with any blessings that you may have received in your life. Resorting to the lowest common denominator, if you have to… "I am blessed with each and everyday! I am blessed to have a healthy and happy family, free from the chains of a tortured childhood! I am blessed to be able to draw breath each and everyday",…

then give thanks!…

VIGNETTE 16

GOOD NEWS!!! YOU
ARE A SUCCESS!!!

My main claim to success in my life is my son, Bernard Junior. My one son and only child. We raised him in pure love. His mother died when he was 7. She loved Bernie Jr. more than life itself!

Having been raised Catholic christian, I hardly ever… I never read the Bible… Good Catholics heard our weekly scripture reading followed by the priest delivering the homily.

My wife, raised Baptist and was well versed in the good book. On her deathbed, she asked that I read the Bible to her… As her dying wish, she had blessed me into doing something that I was extremely reluctant to do.

It was then that I first read the entire Bible from cover to cover! As I worked my way through the old testament, I could see a calming comfort ascend onto her face… When she opened her eyes, it was as if a radiant translucence was glowing from within her… As my own sense in tranquility grew, somewhere in the midst of psalms, I was in awe of the utter beauty and magnificence of the written Word!… With such an eloquent display of allegorical metaphors, at times, it was hard to distinguish between where Heaven ended and humanity began… With the sheer number of "begettings" that were going on and on, it was all I could do to keep from blushing!... PG-13 material... The new testament was the "creme de la creme". Four consecrated men kept hammering home the same "GOOD NEWS"... *He has risen and will come again!...* This was my wife's final request and blessing...

Towards the end of her days, I placed our son's plush bunny rabbit on her deathbed... Clutching our son's bunny, her last spoken word, before going into a chemotherapeutic coma was..., "Bernie"!!!...

Most everytime I greet my son, it's with a kiss on the lips. I see nothing wrong with expressing love, to my son in this manner. Initially, I used to tell him that "this was from your mother". Now, it's just an expression of pure love. *"Love"*,... now there's a word totally unspoken in my childhood...

On my 40th birthday, my father said to me, "this is something that I realize I have never ever told you,... I love you.". It was then that he kissed me on the lips. I knew *this* from my heart of hearts and my earliest childhood memories.

To my utter shock and awed surprise, the fighter pilot's wife told me, for the first time at 50, "I love you but I don't understand why you keep dating emotionally disturbed women?!". Hmmmm... I wonder why?

I had heard her words, yet somehow,... they failed to register. My entire childhood of abuse had cast a long and permanent shadow... Living in that shadow, her words were met with a lifetime of distrust and a great deal of incredulity... In retrospect, it shames me that the thought of reciprocating never even occurred to me...

In our household, there was never any discussions concerning anything to do with the emotional aspects of this "human enterprise"... There was never a conversation or verbal expression of *ANY* emotion. Never a, "how are you feeling? How was your day?"... never a spoken word of love...

Framing it in as nice a context as I can, we had "constitutional parents". All we got was a list of dos and don'ts. As our constitution is a list of prohibitions for government, it was always, "don't slouch at the dinner table, don't chew with your mouth open, don't put your elbows on the table, don't get up unless you are excused, don't forget to brush your teeth, don't run with scissors, don't ride your bike in the streets and oh, most importantly...don't ever leave the house with dirty underwear!".

Till the day the fighter pilot's wife died, I honestly believe she ever realized that she had wronged me in anyway.

It is my belief that *ALL* abusive parents justify their behavior as their proprietorial rights being exercised... I was a fraction of a person and property of the fighter pilot's wife...

> *How unspeakably horrid it must be to go through generations*
> *upon generations as the abused property to another!!!...*

I recall a year or so before she passed, discussing one of my alcoholic brother's shortcomings. In fishing for a backdoor compliment, I reminded her that I had quit drinking when Bernie Jr. was born, 30 years ago.

She looked me straight in the eye and then stoically replied, *"then how do you explain how you turned out?!"*... Remaining true to her form, her sharp tongue continued to slice and dice her only defiant son... At the end of her days she honestly had no inclination as to the damage that she had inflicted. As always, I held *my* tongue in shame...

There has to be an unspoken code of honor among those kids that grow up being tortured! Shame, embarrassment and fear of reprisal mute our voices.

For most of my life, I felt that I would take my experiences to the grave... After a lifetime of silence, introspection, research and self therapy, I felt compelled to share my story. Perchance to help those that have walked in my shoes. Perchance that maybe the 70 plus million adult-children might relate to and benefit from my experiences and insights. Hopefully sharing in my healing process.

I had realized many years into my adult-childhood, that the fighter pilot's wife *was* my mother and that I would have taken a bullet for her...

Somehow, I felt that I would be less of a person by exposing my prepubescent torture... Constantly trying to explain the twisted irony of contempt, inter -twined with the presumption of love, makes for a lifetime of mental turmoil.

My young heart desperately yearned for solace. My immature mind was profoundly confused by this daily contradiction in terms.

- How is it possible to be loved and hated at the same time?

- How could my mother have loved me and shown such naked contempt, exacting an inordinate amount of pain and anguish?!
- How can this oxymoronic quandary *NOT* lead to utter madness?

After many, many years of self study and analysis, I had learned to accept it as a non-issue and have forgiven her for the trauma she had inflicted. Forgiveness in no way shape or manner ever forgets...

Early into my therapy sessions, I was sharing with my therapist that I felt that I might be exaggerating the significance of my toxic childhood traumas. Maybe it's time that I just learn to get over myself and my internal self pity... That I should have just been a better soldier and submitted to my mothers ironclad will, incessant violent beatings and verbal bashings...

I was trying to talk myself out of the need for therapy. My therapist replied that this was a common "stuck-point" for adult children surviving abusive childhoods. Self deprecation and guilt had reared its ugly head!...

I then explained to my therapist that all my life, prior to being diagnosed with PTSD and consequential depression, I had always felt all of our emotions were a *choice.*

I always prided myself to be an "out of the box" thinker, a problem solver. I had asked myself, "what has changed in my life", that I would start to feel fatigued and listless every morning?

I had emptied my nest and was semi-retired.... I had time to contemplate my navel and stare into the deep, dark chasm of my psyche... All that I saw was extremely sad and disparaging...

So I had simply decided not to feel depressed anymore. My therapist smiled and said, with a raised eyebrow, "so you think you can just *will* yourself out of depression?". To which I replied, "you damn skippy!". After all, I am my mother's son... I had inherited her cast iron will and determination. It is proving to be a deliberating work in progress.

All things are possible which pass through the Son of God...

As the sands of time sifted through the hourglass, I had witnessed the fighter pilot's wife's transformation. She had metamorphosed into the loving and incarnate heart of my grandmother. I often wondered if my grandmother had made this same transition… Only God knows…

In time, my mother had become my grandmother!… When it came to her grand and great grandkids, the fighter pilot's wife had a heart *so big*, it was a medical miracle that there was any room left for the rest of her vital organs! I stood witness to her loving and doting over my son, as I had been with her mother.

Forgiveness is the first and most crucial element of healing… *LOVE* is the medicine that will eventually heal all wounds. Love is at the root of all that is good in this human enterprise we call life… It is our last commandment, to… "love one another as I have loved you…". Love is the light of the world… God is the light and the love of the world…

So many of us go through life searching for the answer. As if we were blindly searching in a pitch black cave for a candle that was lit over 2000 years ago.

GOOD NEWS! The candle was never extinguished! It remains lit and radiates brilliantly within us all. God is love and the Holy Spirit within us, if only we would accept Him… and allow Him to shine through…

CONNECTING THE DOTS!

Living with my grandparents through High school, I was witness to my grandpa suffering from extreme chronic pulmonary disease, emphysema.

One morning at our breakfast table, he was wheezing, desperately struggling to breath. My grandma went up to him to lovingly touch his shoulder and console him. Desperately struggling for air, he pushed back on her and bellowed, "Get away from me WOMAN!!!" Grandma coward away into her sewing room. I followed her, kissed her on the cheek, telling her that I loved her.

In retrospect, I realized that this very personal moment had thrown open a window into the dynamics of my mothers life. Mother was the only girl with five brothers, two of whom drank themselves to death,... resulting from PTSD? Only God knows... At this juncture, it would remain a strong point of contingency.

Grandfather was from the old country, Mexico, where stereotypically women are treated like second class citizens. It is my contention that my mother had witnessed, during her childhood an overbearing and domineering father. Displaying exhibitions of misogynism and extreme ALPHA masculine traits towards women was of a normal consequence.

My mother's mother had been raised entirely by Catholic nuns at the turn of the 20th century. There have been entire volumes written about the severe and torturous corporal abuses that went on in these convents... During this time in our history, many young wounded women chose the vows, security and sanctity of the Catholic church to avoid violent and impoverished childhoods.

Considering where they had come from, three hots and a cot were a definite improvement... "Learned behavior" had embedded itself into the holiest of holies, the Catholic church. From this environment was born the folklore of "Sister Mary Elephant", the epitome of brutality and antagonism, the wrath of God!... For generations of unsuspecting and undeserving orphans, the Mea culpa of penance went well beyond prayerful repentance.

It is my contention that the fighter pilot's wife had vowed and was determined to never ever raise sons with any inkling of any ALPHA traits. She had vowed to use whatever methods or force to modify and squash her son's alpha traits and male tendencies.

Something or someone in my mother's childhood had instilled a mean, malicious streak into her persona. She was determined to eviscerate the ALPHA traits in all of her sons. I was her "only" *defiant* son...

It did not serve me well...

Her youngest brother, a Catholic priest, uncle Bernie once confided in me, "your mother has a mean streak in her.". I recall in reminiscence, thinking, "You think! Your not telling me something that I don't already know!". My uncle's assessment of the fighter pilot's wife disposition was somewhat of an understatement...

My entire life's experience held incriminating evidence to the contrary. Her demeanor with her first born son went well beyond mean spirited... Her vile lambastings, coupled with her brutal physical batterings were vicious and malicious. Her methods of control were vindictive and contemptuous... She was extremely vain with an unforgiving heart which was incapable of expressing any kind of love or affection. Her emotional elusiveness was a continuing allure for those of us trying to gain even a modicum of affection. Whenever we went to show her affection with a kiss, she would always turn her cheek. Our starving little hearts were pining for just a modicum of love or affection... With heavy and unfulfilled hearts "We desperately clung to that which was electrocuting us".

Her will to manipulate and emasculate me was relentless!... From the tender age of 3 to a battle weary 12 years of age, I resisted and survived her tyrannical and sociopathic tendencies...

It's by the grace of God and my father's love that I didn't turn out to be a psychopath. Instead, my survival skills were honed, refined and heightened to help me exist and survive an entire childhood firmly imbedded in violent and abusive hostility.

Abused children tend to be extremely observant and intuitive. We are forced to become more apt in developing a social skill set which enhances self preservation. We learn very early on, in a tumultuous lifestyle to lie, beg, borrow and even steal for survival. Being raised in a toxic environment we learn to assimilate in order to be highly judgmental and quick reads of body language.

We learn, literally from "the school of hard knocks" to be insightful and accurate judges of character... Abused children possess a high degree of discernment and an innate ability for rapid-fire deductive reasoning... Traits that are imperative to survival and for self-preservation.

In every social environment, we quickly assess all key players as a potential threat with a predetermined exit strategy at hand. Hypervigilance is rudimentary to those suffering from PTSD... This, in an attempt to be proactive in anticipation of the next "shoe dropping", the "next hammer falling", rather the next "In coming" assaulting onslaught...

Something as simple as a squinted facial eye movement can act as an early detection warning system. Hypersensitivity is crucial in an early warning defense mechanism... Our spidey senses, rather, our cortisol and adrenaline hormones are constantly on *RED* alert!... "Defense condition", DEFCON #1", ready to initiate full defensive measures... This, in and of itself wreaks havoc on our physical health and mental well being...

STRESS BORN FROM TRAUMA KILLS!...

As in the domino theory, stress has a systemic cause and effect relationship on our mental and physical faculties. One domino falls to bring down another, to bring down the next one... Child abuse begets PTSD which begets inordinately high secreations of stress hormone cortisol, which begets depression, which begets any number of esteem and other mental health issues.

On the physical side of this PTSD equation, causation from exposure to excessive stress hormones topples a slew of medical dominos. T2D, hypertension, heart and kidney disease to name the key players. Alcoholism and drug abuse are subsequent antagonistic side effects… They're depressing and destructive nature seeks out and destroys hearts, livers and minds…

Uncle Bernie added that my uncle Joe his oldest brother, had anger issues as did my mother… as do I and some of my siblings… My uncle Felix and uncle Judas both had anger issues, eventually drinking themselves to death…

This, in and of itself, means nothing. Unless it is the underlying symptom from PTSD born from transgenerational abuse.

All signs were pointing to an obvious conclusion… It appears that my mother's abusive behavior was *transgenerational.* At any rate, there is was!

After over 55 years of self-analysis, behavioral deductions and conjecture I was finally able to *connect the dots!*

Mother dearest, It does my heart a world of good to be able to catch just a glimpse beyond your cold, calloused veneer. Therein I am able to distinguish just a glimmer of an unmasked adult child, … wounded in the same manner as my own heart…

Alas,… after years of wading through my own raw psychological nudity…

After nearly a lifetime of searching through the therapeutic minutiae of my life, I was finally able to see a whispered, yet crystal clear glimpse of you. You had been encumbered by the same shackles and chains of "human misery and degradation" as I had been… You had been an unwitting victim to your own circumstances as an abused child…

Postmortem, I had finally found the fighter pilot's wife!…
I had finally FOUND MY MOTHER!!!

Mother dearest,… my anguished heart desperately pines for an alternate universe. A universe wherein I am a loved son and you are my loving mother. It is then and there that my heart swells up and leaps for joy…. The lump in my throat prevents my tears from flowing… sons of warriors aren't permitted.

Therein that alternate existence, the regrets for a life "that might have been" are swept away by the winds of time… The existence in the antithesis of so many missed opportunities in a lifetime filled with the constant fear of retribution,… so much distrust, so much pain, so much disbelief and denial… So many regrets for simply being unable to say that…

"I love you…".

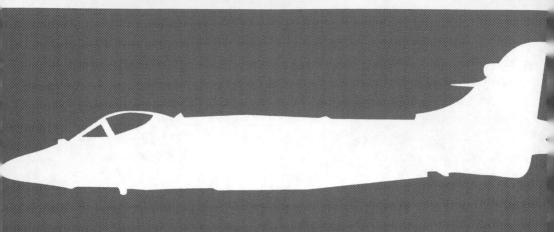

THE INQUIRING MIND

A prerequisite to Self therapy

Cognitive thought processes are key to understanding the unexplainable. Since our entry into this human enterprise, the very nature of our inquiring mind has enabled our species to remain at the top of the food chain. Our ability to use our intellect in logic and reasoning, "cognitive thinking" is what separates us above the rest of the animal kingdom. Our inquiring minds compel us to evaluate so that we may apply what we have learned from our life's experiences...

After leaving University, I intrinsically knew that there was *something seriously wrong with me. This, in and of itself demanded a series of endless self inquiries...*

- *Why do I do things that continually destroy my potential?*
- *Why do I continually look over my shoulder for impending doom?*
- *Why do I feel so helplessly hopeless at times?*
- *Why do I have such a lowly self-esteem, feeling tired and listless?*
- *Why am I reluctant to meet or socialize with strangers?*
- *Why am I scared to death of rejection and meeting girls?*
- *Why is it, that whenever startled, I defensively, raise a forearm?*

- *Why am I reluctant to offer any opinion?*
- *Why do I procrastinate so much?*
- *Why do I feel at my best, alone and in familiar surroundings?*
- *Why have I avoided my family for 8 years, after college? Never realizing it was a "mother avoidance syndrome".*

These are all questions and thoughts that arise from extreme PTSD born from a toxic childhood.

I found myself reading "Psychology Today", from cover to cover, year after year after year, not ever knowing what I was looking for. For eight years of quandary, I felt like a blind man feeling by touch through a haystack for that elusive pin prick.

After several years of study, introspection and soul searching, I started to come out of my social shell. I started contributing to conversations. I started offering feedback in an intelligent and witty manner.

In therapeutic introspection, I realized that I had been using humor, my entire life, as a means to *deflect* attention away from myself. Many adult children live with an overwhelming sense of being wholly inadequate, helplessly and hopelessly flawed... This tends to manifest itself into "antisocial personality disorders" as well as self destructive traits, such as procrastination and other "learned behaviors"...

These are common denominators among abused, adult-children. Very simply put, *abuse destroys self esteem*, which in turn compels us to manufacture self defense mechanisms to cloak our perceived deficiencies.

Think back to all the class clowns in school. A majority of whom acting out to cloak their own tumultuous childhoods. Many of whom were disciplined or even expelled for disrupting class. Some managed to make a successful career of their torment. Ironically, many of whom had met tragic, self induced endings. Yet another example of substance abuse attempting to numb the pain from a tormented childhood...

For example, Robin Williams, depression, John Baluchi, drug overdose and John Candy, food addiction to mention a few. Richard Pryor was a near FLASH in the pan, freebasing... We are all members of the silently tortured, adult children of this world... desperately seeking just a flicker of positive reinforcement.

The dichotomy of a clown helps to illustrate the perplexity of the human mind. Is it any wonder that laughter is a natural painkiller? The effects of the brain chemical, dopamine is as euphoric as opium! On the downside, is it any wonder that so many children and adults are scared to death of such an unnatural display of exaggerated pseudo comedy?

Humor not only *deflects* attention from one's self, it also fulfills our basic need for acceptance. We are all of us, starved for love, approval and affection. The recognition that your wit has brought pleasure to someone, is *intoxicating!* If for only a moment, we feel as if we are... *UNBROKEN*..

My college roommates noticed and commented, "Bernie, your coming out of your shell! Your morphing back into the person we knew in high school". Little by little, my self-esteem was starting to heal.

I was transforming from the shell of a broken introvert and evolving into somewhat of an extrovert. My inner child was attempting to free itself from the shackles of repression and suppression of an abhorrent childhood.

I would eventually become a confident public speaker. My "Dale Carnegie" class awarded me a "public speaker extraordinaire" plaque, inviting me back as an intern instructor.

With a sense of exhilaration from vindication, I began to realize how a life well lived was meant to be.

I was starting to feel more alive and purpose driven... but only to a point. I continued to struggle with "learned behavior" and those God damned "negative tapes". For the rest of my life, I would never realize, until recently, that I had been struggling with chronic and severe PTSD.

At any rate, after connecting the dots going back two generations, I came to this revelation.

The abusive cycle had been extinguished. The buck had stopped with me!

I had severed the insidious, toxic head of transgenerational child abuse.

I swore to myself that if I ever have children, I would never raise a hand to them!... My son has known only love and support his entire life. My life-purpose was to push him up through college and successfully equipped for a life well lived..

He has been successfully launched and is college educated. Bernie Jr. is happily married to a gorgeous, smart, absolutely wonderful young lady-longhorn! Yes, it is a mixed marriage, Aggies and Longhorns… Love conquers all! They are getting ready to make me a grandpa! I'm so proud of him, I could just *SPIT!*

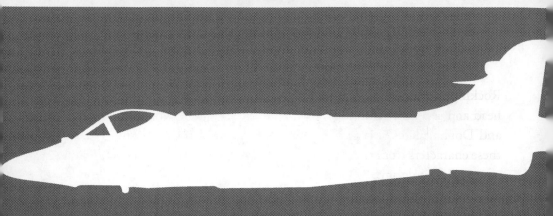

NEUROSIS: EFFECTS OF UNRESOLVED SUFFERING

"A relatively mild mental illness"

Flashing back to the first night of my initial childhood traumatic event, I found myself unable to fall asleep. I recall, actually being afraid of falling asleep for fear of impending doom or that something bad would happen to me while I slept. I would lay awake in bed until all hours of the night.

Without the benefit of hindsight, at 4 years of age, I was experiencing inordinately high levels of anxiety. In a biological response to this anxiety, extremely high secretion levels of cortisol, our stress hormone surges through our brain. A prevalent symptom of PTSD... I had been physically and emotionally traumatised by the person that should have been there to love and nurture me.

Suddenly, rocking myself in a fetal position simply wasn't enough. The redistribution of my stress hormone just wasn't happening. It had been sufficient in coping with the loss of Bunny.

"Splish, splash, WHAM!", had cut too deeply! After several nights of laying anxiously awake, exhaustion would eventually overcome me.

Rocking back and forth with my blanket tucked completely over my little head and shoulders, I would repeat over and over again, "Mickey Mouse and Donald Duck, Mickey Mouse and Donald Duck"... As if invoking these characters from toontown would somehow ward off these sensations of impending doom... From this trepidation was born a rather peculiar and neurotic behavioral pattern.

I would lay on my back, shaking my head from left to right, 180 degrees and back again, over and over and over again. Eventually, I would fall into slumber.

This somehow blocked out all cognitive thinking, all painful thoughts of doom and gloom. Shaking my head with such intensity that my bed would literally slide several feet from the wall. I didn't care. What I couldn't see or think could not hurt me.

This was neurotic behavior brought on by the stress from a severe traumatic event. It was a neurotic behavioral coping mechanism, directly resulting from unresolved suffering and emotional trauma.

Neurosis is a relatively mild mental illness caused by the stress of trauma. The direct result of unresolved pain and suffering.

As a baby is coddled and rocked to redistribute the stress hormone cortisol, my head shaking was achieving this same result. The absence of this process in infants, results in brain damage and ultimately death.

In extreme cases of infant neglect, babies are left in their cribs to die from accumulations of this stress hormone, cortisol in their cortex. Psychiatrists deduced this in orphanages at the turn of the 20th century. We can simply die from the neglect... by failing to rock the cradle...

- Another direct causation from PTSD is type 2 diabetes. In three baseline studies of PTSD survivors, those with more than 3 years of exposure to this stress disorder were more than twice as likely to incur T2D. The longer the exposure to this stress hormone the greater the propensity for T2D. The proclivity for this disease increases exponentially. The cause and effects of stress and the excessive secretion of cortisol in our bodies is detrimental and potentially deadly to our well being. Other detrimental side effects are heart disease, obesity and high blood pressure to name just a few. Complications from T2D brought on by a lifetime of excessive cortisol secretions inevitably leads to kidney failure then death or dialysis… This will be my ultimate quandary… I am merely months away from making this decision… *THE STRESS FROM TRAUMA IS DEADLY!!!*

After a lifetime of extreme PTSD, over 50 years, I had succumbed to hypertension and T2D. Prior to my research, introspection and self discovery and recovery therapy, I used to believe that I was genetically predisposed to T2D and hypertension. Little did I know, my health was predetermined by my exposure to a lifetime of PTSD, born from a toxic childhood and violent maltreatment.

- Yet another manifestation of stress from unresolved suffering is "Bruxism" or grinding and gnashing of your teeth. Usually while asleep but not restricted only to slumber. This is a neurotic symptom of PTSD. A condition brought on by extreme *anxiety and anger* from unresolved suffering. I learned this the hard way. After a lifetime of neurotically grinding my teeth at night, I split three molars in half. Bruxism is described as a neurotic behavior. I recall thinking, " how can this be, I'm not neurotic… *I'm not crazy!*".

This raised yet another *red flag in my mind's eye.* Just one more, of several pieces to my puzzle were starting to fall into place. At any rate, bruxism fractured a few molars, resulting in excruciating pain. I don't recommend it to anyone. A nightly rubber teeth guard was mandated by my dentist.

- An *extremely rare* consequence of anxiety and stress brought on by trauma is Kleptomania. I am mortally chagrined in sharing my most appalling symptom from PTSD induced by child abuse. At the age of 3, after Bunny had been ripped from my life, I found myself procuring incidental and valueless items to somehow justify and offset the loss of Bunny.

I recall the first incident, as I was with my mother visiting a neighbor. As they were chatting and having coffee, I started playing with a tiny

American flag from a coffee table centerpiece. When we got home, mother noticed that I was waving this tiny flag. She asked where I had gotten it.

She was shocked when I told her that I had taken it from our neighbors home. I was just 3 ½ and wasn't aware that I had done anything wrong. I saw it, I wanted it so I simply took it… She sternly ordered me to return it at once. So I did…

Growing up, I continued to find myself taking insignificant trinkets with little or no intrinsic value. This grated on the consciousness of my soul, to the point that I disclosed it in a confessional at around 9 years of age. I thought the priest was going to come out of the confessional to apprehend me!!!

This scared the devil out of me! After all, breaking the 7th commandment was a Cardinal sin! For fear of burning in Hell, I squelched the uncontrollable desire to steal as a means to deal with my loss.

I learned at a very early age that the anxiety from extreme traumatic stress can bend one's moral flexibility…

Neurosis: substitutes for legitimate suffering, was deduced at the turn of the 20th century by psychiatrist Carl Jung. "Facing our deepest, darkest inner secrets rather than letting it manifest into self destructive behaviors", (i.e.learned behavior) was one of Carl Jung's precepts.

I learned this by the extreme chance of researching the symptoms of complex PTSD. The author described many of the same symptoms that I was experiencing. This was the final, missing piece of the puzzle. My "Ah ha" moment, my destiny moment, if you will.

The symptoms of PTSD that were described from a childhood filled with abuse, aligned perfectly with my experiences! "Awakening many mornings, wishing that I hadn't… Those feelings of listlessness and fatigue, even after having slept more than enough"… It made perfect sense!

Ever since my nest was emptied, I had lost my sense of purpose. My constant preoccupation was with work. Hyper productivity is a side effect of an underdeveloped superego…Working with an extreme sense of urgency had come to an end.

I had gotten my son through six years of college. All that I had to do now was to contemplate my navel and stare into the deep darkness of my inner psyche… That short, seemingly inconsequential book was the catalyst that led me to psychotherapy and hopefully to the healing of my mind's eye.

Perchance to silence those damned negative voices!

"Your demons comforted you, when no one else would.
They were holding you when no one else did… Thats
why its so hard to get rid of them!"… unknown.

"You can hate your demons with all that you are. You can yell, scream
and curse them with all heart. But at the end of the day, they're the only
ones that see your scars. When you remove the mask that hides your face,
they're the only ones that really know who you are…"… unknown.

The "walking wounded" anguish in an insidious existence of a desperately lonely world. *An earthly HELL totally void of any empathy or love… I agree with Pope Francis. "There is no HELL…" Hell is simply the existence in the total absence of our Fathers love…* Many of us are living proof that "hell exists here on earth"…

Tormented psyche's are like onions. *What?!…* I know, this is an overly simplified metaphor, yet effective. In therapy, our buried traumas are peeled away, layer by layer until the core is exposed.

Our psyche's have developed layer upon layer of mental anesthesia. This isolates our subconscious thought processes. Acting as a psycho self defense, if you will. Like thick calluses, they protect us from our deepest, darkest most appalling memories. In extreme cases of abuse the separation of our cortex and limbic brain system is a GOD send to our mental survival. We move on to survive as wounded adult-children and socio or psychopaths but we… survive nonetheless…

Isn't God GREAT!?

At any rate, the shaking of my head from side to side was labeled as a neurotic behavioral coping mechanism. My psychotherapist seemed startled, taken- back when I shared this with her. Graciously, she quickly deduced that this was a coping behavior pattern which redistributed the stress hormone, cortisol in my frontal cortex. At the conclusion of our first session, my therapist advised me to use extreme caution in driving home… She could sense the anguish in my shared revelations…

This "head shaking" was soothing as it somehow gave me solace, so that I might be able to fall asleep. This behavior pattern continued throughout my entire childhood and into early adolescence. At fourteen or fifteen, I began to seriously question, "why was I doing this, each and every night?!". This was a conscious prelude to cognitive behavioral therapy… *What the hell is wrong with me?! Am I stupid, crazy or what!?".*

The separation of my limbic system and cortex had buried my trauma deeply into my psyche. As an adolescent-child, I was unable to correlate, remember or connect the dots.

Suppression: *In psychological application, is the act of stopping yourself from thinking or feeling something for self preservation…*

Truth be known, I am mortally ashamed and embarrassed by my entire childhood. I somehow felt that I must have been guilty as charged. It had to have been my fault. Otherwise I wouldn't be on the receiving end of such brutal maltreatment, almost my entire childhood and early adolescence.

WHAT!? How could it have been my fault!? Yet, this is what I felt as a child victim of abuse… This is yet another "stuck point" common among tortured children. As an adolescent child, I simply chose to suppress it… to squash it down and out of sight! Ignorance was bliss!…

This is what a majority of the "walking wounded" believe and do. We were all too innocent to the ways of the world to know any better. We are implicitly incapable of rationalizing or discussing our predicaments. Moreover, we have no one to trust or confide in… All of our shared traumas are *unspeakable* in the society in which we live.

15 years ago, I tried telling the fighter pilot about my childhood… He turned his back on me and simply walked away, never to whisper, nah a single word on this matter again. *Raw denial and refusal to acknowledge the abhorrence of the truth was on full display…*

The world of tortured children is an abhorrently *private* and a *horribly lonely* state of being!

Therein, a majority of suicides come as a complete and total shock to those closest to the victims. For the most part, those left behind are blindsided...

Those tell tale hearts are forever silenced,... as they simply die from secrecy.

In the midst of many, invariably... *we are all alone...* This is why *90%* of all tortured children live in silent anguish... We fumble through a silent, desperate, guilt ridden existence.

Our only reliable companions are the disparaging demons who constantly shadow us. They are ever present. They *cling* to us... keeping us from being totally and solitarily confined to loneliness.

We are desperately isolated in an oxymoronic embrace. Our demons exude a *cruel comfort,* pulling at us from a perpetual darkness,... Clinging to us and deceitfully coaxing us towards the dismal shadows of depression. When will they ever be silenced?...

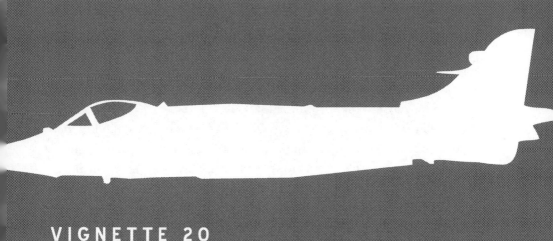

VIGNETTE 20
"BERNIE TERRIFIC"

ZZZzzzzzzz...

After my initial traumatic event, (splish, splash, wham!) eventually I was able to achieve REM sleep. My surroundings were that of a much more tranquil world. I could sense a soothingly warm glow, as my dream state was totally void of any suffering or angst.

It was always at the equinox to the twilight of the day, when the dusk kisses the sun goodbye. The top two thirds of the skyline was always pitch black. The horizon was a glimmering reddish orange, fading to black. It was there that I always found myself in a familiar urban environment.

Little by little, shadows grew longer and the glare of dusk was eventually consumed by total darkness. Therein, something black and ominous was lurking... As my breathing became labored, I could feel my heart beating with increased regularity.

Suddenly and without forewarning I would sense a warm glow in my tummy! As it intensified, I actually felt myself starting to levitate off the ground! Eventually just high enough to avoid the impending evil beneath me.

I had no idea what was down there.. Intrinsically, I sensed that if I didn't levitate, I would be devoured. All I knew, is that whatever was down there, it was evil and that it wanted me…

As the glow in my tummy intensified, I would fly higher and higher and out of harm's way. As the night completely consumed the daylight, I could, ever so faintly hear a guttural grumbling. It was a lulled murmure, gnashing of teeth and growling beneath my feet. I was never able to see it… but could sense something very dark and ominous down below me.

I was never able to fly higher than the rooftops of our USAF community, just high enough to remain out of harm's way. *I was FREE!* Free, at last from all pain and suffering…

All the neighborhood kids exclaiming, "Hey, look! Bernie can fly!" "Isn't Bernie terrific!?". Yes!… I was like Peter Pan, jumping from rooftop to rooftop! I *was* "Bernie Terrific"! The warm glow in my tummy was accentuated by the admiration and accolades from my peers.

It felt so good to be praised and acknowledged! "Bernie Terrific" would stay with me for over 10 years…

He felt like a lifelong buddy and friend, from 4 years of age to 14 or 15… "Bernie Terrific" was an elusive escape artist. Always narrowly avoiding nipping at his heels. Always evading impending doom in the nick of time. "Bernie Terrific" was my subconscious bed-buddy.

He constantly helped in coping with the reality of my childhood. Each and every night was an adventure in avoiding the "jaws of malevolence". The exuberance of avoiding *vicious ill will,… somehow made my life seem bearable…*

The euphoria and freedom from impending doom was intoxicating. It was a welcome reprieve from those dark, haunting voices. It was as if I had been temporarily pardoned from a lifetime yoke of physical, psychological and emotional pain.

Finding myself unable to truly soar like a bird, was the manifestation of my "learned behavior". My entire life I was limited from ever truly achieving success,… truly soaring.

At any rate, "Bernie Terrific" was a much welcomed companion. To escape the realities of a tortured childhood, if only in *JUST* a dream… "Bernie Terrific" would remain a constant, soothing sidekick, throughout prepubescents and into the onset of my early adolescence.

As "Puff the Magic Dragon" left when "little Jackie Paper" grew out of childhood, so went "Bernie Terrific". "Dragons live forever, but not so little boys. Painted wings and giant strings make way for other toys. One grey night, Jackie Paper came no more.". Puff hung his head in sorrow. That mighty dragon, sadly slipped into his cave. Ohhhh... Puff the magic dragon bid farewell from the land on Honalee!

The magic of youth had *forever* gone away, if only in a dream. Little Bernie terrific had slipped away... I would miss that little rascal!

In my coming of age, "Bernie Terrific's" disappearance coincided with the concerted effort to stop my neurotic, behavioral head shaking. One grey night the music stopped and the magic went away, this along with the shaking of my head to sleep, each and every night. I would miss that rascal "Bernie Terrific"...

At 14 or 15 years of age, I recall thinking,"if I ever get married, my wife will think I'm crazy!".

I wasn't crazy. just trying to cope with unresolved pain.

Truth be known, I was a *SUCCESS!!!* My son, Bernie Jr. is my *OPUS* and my life's masterpiece. Getting him through six years of college, at one of the best universities in the world, is my claim to fame.

In his youth, I used to tell him, jokingly that he was a piece of work... He *IS* my life's work and most certainly the best thing I have ever done!

Bernie truly is TERRIFIC!

Fast forward to early in my therapy sessions. I shared "Bernie Terrific" with my therapist. She complimented me on my ability to develop such an effective coping mechanism and at such a young age. Our subconscious enables us to contrive self medicating dream states to help offset the negative effects from trauma.

That very next night, I dreamt that I was flying, for the first time in nearly 50 years. The setting was exactly as I had remembered.

Suddenly, I noticed I wasn't able to gain enough elevation to avoid the dark impending doom below me. Stark, cold terror gripped me as I realized that something black was panting at my heels! Too late!!!...

Up from the darkness, this huge black German Shepherd leaped up to my eye level and laid a big, sloppy, slurpy doggy kiss on my face. Suddenly, all fear of impending doom had dissipated…

In sharing my "Bernie Terrific" dreams with my therapist, my cognitive thought processes enabled me to rationalize the slumbering fear stored in my limbic system.

Up from the depths of my hippocampus came the memories from my childhood dreams nearly 50 years earlier. Cognitive behavioral therapy had placed my childhood fears into a rationally benign state of being.

When I described my dream to my therapist, as a breakthrough, I could see a smile avail itself onto her lips.

Our human mind, has the innate ability to recover and heal itself. The human consciousness is capable of rationalizing and defusing trauma by varying degrees . A hundred billion neurons, electrochemically charged, enable us to unlock the mysteries of our minds and the universe.

VIGNETTE 21

THANK GOD FOR THE LOVE OF OUR FATHER!

Life at our father's military Academy had its share of pleasant memories. I attended two bonfires for the first time in my young life. The yell practices and cadet student body exuberance was overwhelming. While there as an undergraduate, father had to work part time at the campus theatre to help pay for his education. During his undergraduate years, mother worked full time at the city's utilities. Her gainful employment was instrumental to the fighter pilots graduation, not to mention feeding our hungry mouths.

Supplementally, he was hired by his calculus professor to tutor football players. On one occasion, after concluding an engineering calculus math session with a 350 pound, caucasian tackle, he looked to his mentor and exclaimed. "Boy, you're a smart Mexican, aren't ya?".

In the mid fifties, academia was prominently lily white, a sign of our times. The cadet's non-response was appropriate and expected. Having lived all of my brief and sheltered life on air force bases, I was inoculated from bigotry and racism. We were lucky enough to experience the richness of friends from all nationalities and all over the world.

Living in a civilian population, we were exposed to the harsh realities of social ignorance. At a young age, we were witness to its symptoms.

Lt. Fighter pilot took me and my little brother, Felix to pick up the fighter pilots "outsourced" laundry. We drove passed the proverbial railroad tracks. I notice the deterioration in the quality of construction as we continue eastward.

The road turned from asphalt to gravel and eventually to dirt. The homes went from brick and mortar to wood slats. They were now tin and press-board shacks.

We parked at the front steps of a home which by today's standards, would have been condemned. Up some broken and cracked concrete steps to a shanty elevated on cinder blocks. We knocked on a door which didn't seem to align up with it's frame.

An extremely frail and elderly dark woman came to the door and invited us in. I remember the unlevel floor sloping up at an angle as we creaked across one of the two rooms of her abode. The familiar fragrance of boiling beans, ham hocks and lard stimulated my salivary glands.

She gave the fighter pilot several beautifully laundered, starched and ironed shirts. He thanks her by shaking her bony hand, placing therein it a wad of cash. She seemed very pleasant and appreciative.

My eyes were widened to an abhorrent symptom of a prevalent socio-economic inequality. Our short visit awoke a sense of melancholy and newly enhanced appreciation of our own circumstances.

Our father would make his nightly rounds. First to the girl's room to tuck in then kiss on the lips good night. He would tuck in Beatrice, his favorite daughter, Anna and then Suzy. Making his way to the boy's room where he would kiss and tuck in the same loving manner.

First was his youngest and favorite son, his frenchie, Joey then Felix and then myself, Bernard. It did my heart good to see such a display of love and affection! It matters not that father had his favorites. All that matters is that we received love and affection from at least one of our parents. *I thank God for the love of our Father!*

I recall with reluctance the night that I exclaimed to my father that I felt I was getting too big for being kissed. At 4 ½, I was trying to impress him with my maturity... He looked a bit surprised, paused,... then said okay. I have regretted this act of self deprivation my entire life...

Our father was a quintessential contradiction in terms. By day, he was flying the skies in a multi-million dollar instrument of mass destruction, trained to kill our enemies, foreign or domestic. By night, he was 180 degrees at the opposite end of the human spectrum. Lt. Fighter pilot was a loving, affectionate husband and father to his pride. We all waited with pining hearts for his daily return.

Such a paradox in character exemplifies the positive duality of man. Our father's nature was as loving as our mother's should have been. The fighter pilot's wife was every bit the enforcer, illustrating the negative aspects of that same duality.

Our fathers duty was that of a highly trained, professional killer. This confusing dichotomy displays the paradox whenever man is trained as an instrument of war. His order of priorities were; God, country and family. Country was synonymous with duty. Duty and honor were one in the same.

Our father's ability to compartmentalize and separate his professional persona from his family life was extraordinary. His philosophical key to life is self-realization. "Know thyself!" Something that I would be unable to do for most of my adult life. Self-realization, without all the constraints of society was at the foundation of the fighter pilot's philosophy.

As time in our lives progressed we felt proud to see underclassmen snap to attention and sharply salute our father's presence. We were proud to claim him as our own. Thank God for him! Without my father's love, God only knows how I might have turned out...

FAREWELL TO "THE FIGHTER PILOT'S WIFE"...

As every Queen has her reign, invariably she must die… Thus restoring the natural order of things. Completing her earthly cycle of life, our Queen transcends to her next realm …

As my mother lay on her deathbed, I whispered into her ear, "thank you for being my mother and thank you for being such a wonderful grandmother to my son, Bernie Jr.". As she heard Bernie's name, she whimpered in her semi-comatose state.

As I had mentioned earlier, I honestly don't believe that mother ever realized that she had wronged me in anyway. The fighter pilot's wife had to have had a moral flexibility, deeply immersed in denial,… be that as it may.

It is what it was… Well into my adult-childhood, I learned to accept that my mother was a product of her own childhood experiences. All the signs from that generation where glaringly apparent… Forgiveness was absolutely necessary in beginning my healing process.

At her memorial, I gave a 25 minute eulogy, accentuating her positive attributes, making a concerted effort to steer clear of her darkside and glaring contradiction in her personality… We are all complicated individuals… Please allow me to share a few excerpts:

"...not only was mother drop dead gorgeous, she was extremely intelligent as well! She turned heads all over the world. Consequently, it was impossible to win a debate with her.

The beauty of argument, is that if one argues correctly, you're never wrong. By segwaying to an unrelated topic for which there is no disputing, one can throw your opponent into a defensive posture. A subjective counterpoint can be virtually unchallengeable. It matters not that the argument has been diverted to an unrelated topic. All that mattered was that you had shown your opponent in the light of uncertainty.

This might work on the average bear, but not mother! I was constantly debating her, my entire prepubescent and early adolescence. She had an extremely sharp wit, with the ability to think and manuevor quickly on her feet. Everytime I tried to divert the argument to gain tactical advantage, she would very blandly reply, "and what does that have to do with the price of rice in China?".

Mother had a very keen sense of smell. She could smell Bravo Sierra from a mile away. Thats code for B.S., which is an acronym for bull s..., well, you know what I mean. Mother had a keen sense of B.S., and I was full of it! She would have made an excellent special prosecutor. Lord knows, she spent a lot of her life prosecuting me, and I was always found... guilty as charged!

She was the personification of style, grace and beauty. She was the bee's knees, the cat's meow, the quintessential alpha woman of our time. She was as tough as blue steel and had a higher threshold for pain than any mortal that I had ever met.

She would drag herself through shards of glass to protect her children! Case in point, once upon a time, it was Montana, in the dark of night and the midst of a blizzard. She drove herself to the hospital with a ruptured appendix... Major Fighter pilot was called from his fighter interceptor squadron to be at her side. We almost lost her... What more could be said?".

"Before I step down from this podium, I'd like to thank each and everyone for coming to pay homage to our mother. I have just one question for you.

Do you love your mother!? Well,... of course you do!... Okay, prove it… PROVE IT!… (pregnant pause), Well, there IS no empirical evidence, yet you know that it exists. You can feel it in your heart!…

"LOVE"… Love is the only thing that transcends all the laws of physics throughout all of the universes. "LOVE"…, it was the last commandment from Jesus Christ Himself. *"Love one another as I have loved you"*… I believe that we take it with us. Love is the light that we seek throughout our entire lives.

Many of us go through life as if we are blindly searching through a dark cave, looking for a candle that was lit more than 2000 years ago.

GOOD NEWS! It was never extinguished! Search no more! Love is the LIGHT! God is LOVE! Jesus Christ is the LIGHT of the world! Through the powers of deductive reasoning, I have just proven the existence of GOD!…

Mother's love always taught us that true faith requires not the evidence of proof…

Growing up, mother would tell us, never ever paint or scar our bodies in the name of vanity. Our bodies are vessels for the holy spirit. In seeking GOD, with true faith, one has only to look to our inner selves. "You are beacons of light for the lost and the faint of heart.".

Mother was more Catholic than the Pope himself! I know this because once upon a time in our lives, after having had eight kids, she declared, "the Pope can go to hell, I'm taking the pill!… What I do with my body is between me and my Lord!…" Yes, mother had an ironclad will! (Boy did I ever know this!…).

Once again, before I leave you, I thank you for allowing me to share a few microcosms of my life. It is my sincerest wish that you have a better idea of who my mother was. The sum total of what I have shared with you today spell just one word; Mother! Maaaam! Mama!… I miss my mommy…"

"This is bravo sierra, over and out"…

It's been four years since she has left us. In two weeks, I will be in my twelfth month of weekly psychotherapy sessions. Looking forward to completing my "cognitive behavioral therapy" and the silencing of all those *freaking* negative tapes.

After a great deal of thought and consideration, I came to the conclusion that there is no completion to CBT… The end game is merely the search. There is no reprieve from those dark haunting voices… Only the quest to somehow someway rationalize one's existence.

It has been said, that when death smiles upon you, all a man can do is spit in his eye and smile back… As a man sees the end of his life draw near, he desperately wants to know that it counted for something. That his existence on this big beautiful blue marble suspended in darkness has made a difference. He tries to view the sum total of his existence as more than a seemingly random sequence of events. The mere accumulation of inconsequential gadgets, fixtures and assets portrays a certain shallowness, void of anything which is inherently human…

It is then that the thought of my most precious and beautiful grand-daughter, makes my heart leap for joy from within my chest! The very sight of my gorgeous "daughter by law" enter acting with pure unconditional love and affection for my "pookie" makes my heart burst in exultation!… In their presence I find myself smiling soooo much that my face starts to hurt… "My Belle" is the perfect personification of a mothers love which I so desperately pined for my entire life…

The sheer exuberance of a life well lived can be measured by the infinite level of love for family. The full measure of a "life well lived" can best be seen through the prism of "LOVE"… This will prove to be my greatest and most enduring legacy…

Towards the end of her days, the fighter pilot's wife admonished me in a rather judgmental vain, "Why do you always wear black?". I replied enigmatically, "To mourn for all the suppressive and degradative souls in our world…". She retorted that it was so dark and sinister, to which I responded, "Mother, priests wear black…". She had no response and no idea I was mourning for all the abusers on the darkside of her realm. "…turn the other cheek."… Touche'…

My entire adult-childhood has been spent mourning and recognizing the oppressed and tortured children that unceremoniously kerplop into this unforgiving world. My intent has been to shine a brilliant light onto a stereotypically dark and foreboding topic. To know of them and understand their desperately anguished plight is to love them unconditionally… It is for the demeaned and degridated, the tortured and murdered babies that I write this excruciating dissertation...

Often, I find myself gazing into an unrealized potential, then wondering how my life might have turned out with a normal childhood... For the chance of self realization much earlier in my life. For the chance of having felt the warm, nurturing embrace of a mother's affection. Longing, perchance to bask in the glow of a mother's perpetual love... As my aching heart gently weeps, I recite...

"God grant me the serenity to accept the things I cannot change. Courage to change the things I can and the wisdom to know the difference."

My faith and my family's well being is all that I need and cherish.

I fully realize that there will be those that question my lack of credentials. Perhaps even casting dispersions on my psychological conclusions and assessments, dismissing them as some kind of massive rationalization. Especially on a topic that our society evades like the plague. Mental illness carries with it an extremely negative, social stigma of avoidance.

"Who me!? I'm not even slightly mentally ill! Neurotic?!... No way! I'm not weak-minded! I'm not CRAZY! PTSD happens ONLY to wounded warriors....".

These are all, deeply rooted sentiments and misconceptions shared by nearly everyone. It has been my intention to shine a blinding spotlight onto the deep, dark depths of a tortured and tormented psyche... my own.

- *To* give a voice to and amplify the muted, anguished cries of the "walking wounded"... our tortured kids.

- *To* offer up, just one possible, preemptive educational solution to the social pariah of *transgenerational child torture and emotional disembowelment...*

- *To* expose and acknowledge the cold, cruel heart of *transgenerational "child abuse"* and the absolute necessity of severing its toxic, hidiously ugly head...

- *To* perhaps, in just the tiniest of ways, help *destigmatize the extreme negativity of mental illness...*

- *To* correlate the cultivation of psychotic mental illnesses with the mass murder of our children and society in general...

- *To* correlate and expose the danger of the *"extreme political insanity of polarizing partisanship"* and its *direct* contribution to mass, murderous psychopaths...

- *To* explain in layman's terms, how our brains are wired. How our minds cope and function in the midst of tormented, psychological chaos.

I graduated from "The University of Hard Knocks", mastering in "Learned Behavior". I survived and tried to excel in a lifelong struggle with severe and chronic symptoms of *Posttraumatic Stress Disorder, with its genesis in toxic child abuse.*

My entire life has been a constant struggle to cope, in silent desperation. I have stumbled through an impenetrable fog of despair, guilt and regret. Underwriting a lifetime dissertation of "unresolved suffering", where neurotic behavioral coping mechanisms have been my norm.

Having lived a life of introspection, self study and self-psychoanalysis, I ultimately realized that I am who I am. I am a product of my environment and that I am loved by my *Father, who art in heaven.* I am also loved by he who I am the fruit and flesh of his own loins... *my Dad.* I am my father's son... and the product of a transgenerationally abused mother figure.

I make no apologies for my faith and my belief in God the Father, HIs Son and the Holy Spirit...

I was an abused child...

*However, that does not define who I am. I grew to be an adult-child,
a loving husband, a loving father and now a loving grandfather.
Living in the dark shadows of parental complacency, strained moral
flexibility and plausible deniability... I fell victim to the complete
and total delegation of my childhood mismanagement...*

I have *unknowingly* suffered a lifetime with the angst from the "mental disorder", PTSD... Wandering through the *gloom of self degradation*, constantly trying to squelch the anguish and anger of my "inner child". *I can read and I can think, therefore I am...*

These are my qualifications...

This is an impassioned narrative of love, written for all abused children from all time and continuum... written by an abused child...

Thus, I begin my new life, at the twilight of my existence. Inasmuch as I have a finite and extremely limited time left in this world, it is my sincerest desire to have conveyed somewhat of a riveting and unvarnished portrayal of my life's events.

My life, insearch of the "fighter pilot's wife"...

It is my hope that you or someone you know may benefit. To possibly, take what I have experienced and apply to your own lives. It is my genuine desire that you might have that "Ah ha!!!"... destiny moment, *much earlier* in *your* life than I did.

Please know that exposing the minutiae of my "psychological nudity" has chagrined me beyond words. In getting my hands dirty, down in the "psychological weeds", it has been my intention to have openly displayed all of my deepest, darkest and most appalling secrets. If then and only then, if you have benefited in the tiniest of ways, I have succeeded in my wildest dreams.

It is my sincerest prayer that you may have found just an iota of socially redeeming value on my odyssey of recovery therapy. May we all rediscover the magic in our lives... May we all make the most of our lives with the cards we have been dealt... Thanks for coming along for the ride of my life in search of the fighter pilot's wife...

May the good Lord hold you, keep you, cradle you, and rock you...

back and forth, back and forth,... back and forth... All the days of your lives.

End of this process...

This series of vignettes chronicles one person's journey of self discovery, up from the deep, dark depths of a tormented psyche. It's sole intent is to shine a blinding spotlight onto the insidious nature of toxic child torture. Illustrated by the exposure of a disturbingly detailed and brutally honest vision of a life, a life in search of the "fighter pilot's wife".

Who the author is and his life's circumstances are of no consequence. His intent is to;

- Giving a voice to the muted and abused multitudes who have endured much more ghastly, untold stories are at the forefront of his intentions.
- Giving a voice to the violated victims of this country's most appalling, silent but deadly transgenerational tendency is at the heart of this quick read.
- Giving a voice and maybe some perspective and clarity to the 20%. Those 1 in 5 of all Americans that have been victims of the unspeakable atrocities of PTSD born from child abuse, all the adultchildren of our country.

Standing witness to the horrors of war, is a minuscule percentage to those suffering from PTSD. PTSD with it's genesis from a toxic traumatically abusive childhood is much more pervasive in our society and throughout our history.

Posttraumatic stress disorder is a normal consequence from an abnormal cause and effect, brought on by child abuse. There is *never* anything more grotesquely abhorrent than the torturing of a child. Where is the decried response?! Where is the moral outrage?! We are physically, emotionally and psychologically torturing and murdering our own children!!! The collective moral outcry should be as great as if not greater than the #movement "me too"...The side effects from undiagnosed PTSD are physically and mentally detrimental and even deadly.

BERNIE TERRIFIC

From extreme mental trauma, a slew of other psychosomatic and life threatening disorders are born. The authors unvarnished accounts portray, in layman's terms how our minds and brains are wired to cope with the psychological chaos of severe trauma and stress born from child abuse.

ABOUT THE AUTHOR

*B*ernie Terrific, the authors pseudonym, begins his new life, at the twilight *of his life. He chooses to remain anonymous to avoid family ostracism and any undeserved claims of attention grabbing… More importantly, my reluctance to pursue written releases from a rather large and extensive surviving family makes my anonymity imperative. My publisher insists that the absence of said releases would open us up to legal liability. Apparently, my childhood was too egregious to truthfully publish all the players concerned. Hence, all the characters names and geographics have been changed to protect the innocent…*

The author's sincerest intent is giving a voice to the seventy to eighty million adult-children (every generation) to those reticent reflections of abused kids. Exposing the extremely detrimental side effects of PTSD born from child abuse is paramount to this motive.

At 62 years of age, he has had an "Ah haaa!" destiny moment after researching this forbidden topic. It is his utmost wish that his unvarnished expose may lead you to your "Ah haaa!" destiny moment much sooner in your life than he did in his…

Bernie Terrific has led a rather nondescript life and at countless times, a lesson in futility. He has incessantly struggled his entire life with undiagnosed symptoms from extreme PTSD. Most notably, *"learned behavior"* had unknowingly stifled his potential, leading to a lifelong exercise in the frustrating shadows of failure and mediocrity. His entire life has been an effort to "fail forward"…

Bernie's lifelong odyssey of recovery therapy and self enlightenment has led to self affirmation. The realization that *"I can read, I can think, therefore I am"*. The self realization that we are capable of walking our way to self help and eventually therapeutic resolution.

If you were an abused child or know someone who might have been, it would behoove you take in this relatively short read… Finally a book written about abused children by an abused child. If you suffer from grief, depression, self deprecation born from child abuse, you are probaby suffering from PTSD… If you are easily aroused, angered or are prone to anxiety, no matter what the cause, won't you please come walk with him, "Insearch of the fighter pilot's wife".

Printed in the United States
By Bookmasters